LAND ENTRIES
of
GUILFORD COUNTY
NORTH CAROLINA
- 1779-1796 -
and
ROCKINGHAM COUNTY
NORTH CAROLINA
- 1790-1795 -

Compiled by:
Dr. A.B. Pruitt

Southern Historical Press, Inc.
Greenville, South Carolina

Please direct all correspondence and book orders to:
www.southernhistoricalpress.com
or
SOUTHERN HISTORICAL PRESS, Inc.
1071 Park West Blvd.
Greenville, SC   29611

Southernhistoricalpress@gmail.com

Originally Copyright: Albert Bruce Pruitt, 1987
Copyright Transferred 2026 to:
    Southern Historical Press, Inc.
ISBN #978-0-94499-206-7
Printed in the United Sattes of America

Introduction

This book contains abstracts of land entries in (a) Guilford County, North Carolina from November 1779 to December 1796 and (b) Rockingham County from December 1790 to January 1795. The Guilford entries found in the North Carolina Archives in two books: (a) the entries from 1779 to 1795 (numbered in this book from 1855 through 2790) are under Secretary of State Land Entries (Guilford County) (call number SS 954.4); and (b) the entries in this book (numbered from 2791 through 2969) are under Secretary of States Entry Taker's Returns (call number SS 561) have a copy of this book. The Rockingham entries (numbered R89 through R265 in this book) are found in two very small books in the Archives (call numbers SS 964.1 and 964.2). It will be noticed that both these counties have suffered from a loss of entry records. Guilford lost the first 1854 entries when the British burned them. Rockingham lost the first 88 entries for an unexplained reason. The Guilford County book SS 954.4 above has an index in the front of the book listing only the enterers. This index is keyed to the page numbers (not the entry numbers). Also there are a few small variations in spelling of names between the index and the body of the book. I have tried to include these variations in my book; see entries 2557 and 2561 for example of Forbush/Forbes. The pages of the first Guilford County book have been laminated. The same has not been done for the loose pages of Guilford County entries or to the Rockingham County books. None of these books is available on microfilm in the Archives' Microfilm Room.

Guilford County was formed in 1770 from Rowan and Orange Counties; Rockingham County was formed in 1785 from Guilford County. Part of Guilford was also separated in 1779 to form Randolph County. Earlier records for the land mentioned in this book may be found in Orange, Granville, and Rowan Counties.

An entry is a claim made to the appointed entry taker by the enterer for vacant or unclaimed land which was technically the property of the State. The enterer described the land--number of acres, nearby waterways, and neighboring land holders. If there were no problems, the entry taker issued a warrant to the county surveyor to survey the land. The warrant and survey may also describe the land and give additional land marks not mentioned in the original entry.   The warrant and completed survey were sent to the Secretary of State.   A grant or patent was then issued, and the person receiving the grant usually had about twelve months to register the grant in the county.

However, problems or counter claims did often appear. Some of these problems were:
(1) A "caveat" could be issued (after the entry and before the grant) to stop the grant from being issued.   The person making a caveat could say he already owned part or all of the land.   The entry taker usually indicated in the entry book if a caveat was made against all or part of an entry an entry and who made the caveat. Then a jury would settle the dispute.   This decision could be: (a) in favor of the caveater in which case the entry was void or discontinued or the enterer withdrew the entry and the caveater did nothing more; or (b) in favor of the caveater for part of the entry and the caveater retained his part of the land and the enterer obtained a grant for the remainder; or (c) in favor of the caveater and the caveater made a later entry on the land and obtained a grant; or (d) in favor of the enterer so he gets a grant for the land.
(2) After the entry was made and the warrant issued, the surveyor may encounter problems finding enough vacant land.   This problems was usually resolved by changing the entry so the number of acres matched the survey.   The entry taker often made corrections in the entry book in the case of shortages by writing the new number on top of the original entry.
(3) Fees were required to cover the entry, warrant, survey, & grant. If any fee was not paid, the entry was usually discontinued or abandoned and the land was still "vacant" for someone to claim. This later claim may be (a) by a later numbered entry or (b) by using the same entry number and the entry taker wrote the new name on top of the original name.
(4) In addition to the above problems, the entry taker may have made normal mistakes while writing in the entry book.   So some "write overs" indicated in my abstracts may be due to entry taker's error and some may be due to problems encountered during the process of obtaining the grant.

Prior to 1777 obtaining land in North Carolina was not well organized.   Records of land grants survive in the Secretary of State's Office; only rarely the land entries for these grants mentioned in county court records.   The land entry system in

North Carolina was better organized by a law passed in 1777 by the General Assembly.   Under this law one entry taker was to be appointed in each county.   It was under this law that the land entries in this book were made.   There are later land entries (in the NC Archives) for Guilford and succeeding counties into the 1900s.   Most of the later entries are on loose sheets of paper and are for various time periods or one entry per page.

        In my abstracts, I have tried to adhere to the following format:
(a) Entry number; consecutive numbers were assigned to entries on p. 62-74 for indexing purposes; most of these entries are on loose pages.
(b) Date of the entry.
(c) Name of person making the entry or claim; number of acres; and description of the land (usually) in this order: waterways, neighboring land owners (following the word "border"), roads, etc, and an indication   if any "improvement" was mentioned.
The punctuation is almost entirely mine and is included to aid the reader and divide the parts of entry into the areas described above.

        If you find an "interesting" land entry, please write the Land Office (part of the Secretary of State's Office) NOT the North Carolina Archives.   Give the person's name and county because that's how the information is filed there.   If the grant was completed, there will probably (but not always) be a copy of the warrant for survey and the survey in the Land Office.   The warrant often gives information quite similar to the land entry. The survey is more valuable in locating the land and usually is a map giving compass directions and distances between the corners. The chain bearers are often mentioned on the survey but neighboring land holders aren't mentioned as often.   Using the entry, warrant, & survey, it is much easier to find the land and determine you have the correct grant when the number of acres change after the original entry.

        If you know a person owned land in Guilford or Rockingham County, do not despair if you don't find an entry for him in this book.   Many entries were made when the land was a part of Orange, Granville, or Rowan Counties.   Very few of the entries prior to 1778 survive in an of these three counties.   But the warrant and/or survey may exist in the Land Office (part of the Secretary of State's Office--not the Archives).   Or the grant may survive in the Land Office or county deeds.   So, the entry may be lost, but the grant might still exist.   When writing the Land Office, send the person's name and county or counties where he lived because that's how the information is filed.

Please refer to <u>North Carolina Research Genealogy and Local History</u> by H. F. M. Leary and M. R. Stirewalt for additional information about land entries and the land granting process in North Carolina.   This book also contains a dictionary of legal terms often encountered in genealogical work as well as almost everything a genealogist needs to know about North Carolina research.

The map with accompanies this book is included to help the reader locate the creeks which are mentioned most often in the index.   The creek locations are not meant to be exact.   More complete and accurate maps of the counties can be obtained from the North Carolina Department of Transportation or in a book of maps for all North Carolina counties from County Maps (Puetz place, Lyndon Station, WI).   Also the North Carolina Archives sells a set of maps including maps of the state for 1775, 1808, and 1833.   Perhaps the best single maps for Guilford and Rockingham Counties have been produced by Custom House (Box 549, Jamestown, NC); on these maps the early land holders are located along with the date of their grant or land purchase.

A separate index has been provided for each section of this book.   The numbers in the index are the entry numbers, not the page numbers.   At the end of each index is a section devoted to geographical place names, i.e. creek, rivers, fords, mills, etc.

The author wishes to thank the North Carolina Archives for preserving this book and thank the staff for their courteous retrieval of the book from the stacks.   He would also like to thank the people who brought forth affordable computers, printers, and software without which the preparation of this book would have been much more arduous.

Guilford County, NC, Land Entries 1779-1796

[on cover] "Transcript of the Land Entry Books of Guilford Co Book A. Rec. Jul. 27, 1796 Wm Hill."

[Index in front of book for persons entering land which is keyed to the page number, not the land entry number. Sometimes the name is not spelled the same in the index as it is in the land entry.]

page 1
1855. Nov. 16, 1779 William Woods enters 100 ac in Guilford Co on both sides of Mile Br of Balues Cr; border: on W by his own former entry.

1856. Nov. 16, 1779 Joshua Hannah enters 60 (write over) ac on waters of Balues Cr in Guilford Co; border: his own former entry on S, William Bostick on W, & George Pearson on E.

1857. Nov. 16, 1779 Robert Peasley enters 100 ac in Guilford Co on waters of Rock Cr; border: his own land, Shearer's conditional line, & Shearer's dividing line.

1858. Nov. 16, 1779 Bromfield Ridley enters 200 ac in Guilford Co on waters of Hogans Cr and Little Troublesome Cr; border: John Allen, John Hodge, Thomas McCullock, & William Donn's entry.

1859. Nov. 16, 1779 David Cooper enters 640 ac on waters of Allimance and Shockleys Creeks in Guilford Co; border: on N by late survey of John McBride, on W by deeded land of George Goble, on S by John Philip Clap, & on E by Michael Shatterlings.

1860.   Nov. 16, 1779 John McKimic enters 450 ac in Guilford Co on Moores Cr; border: Robinson's deeded land.

1861. caveated by Benjamin Britain; withdrawn.   Nov. 16, 1779 James McKimic enters 500 ac in Guilford Co on both sides of Reedy fork; border: James Hays' old line; includes improvement Benjamin Brittain lives on.

page 2
1862. Nov. 16, 1779 Justam (or Jestion) Knott enters 290 ac in Guilford Co on waters of Blews Cr; border: on W of his own & John Woodside's line, on N by vacant land, on E by William Williams & James Kinman, & on S by vacant land.

1863. Nov. 16, 1779 Justian Knott enters 500 ac on waters of Blews Cr and Haw R in Guilford Co; border: surveyed land of Woods, George Cummins, Joseph Blair, his own land, George Brice, & John Strain.

1

1864. Nov. 16, 1779 Adam Starr enters 200 ac in Guilford Co on S side of Great Allimance Cr; border: his own deeded land on N and his former entry on W.

1865. Nov. 16, 1779 Adam Starr enters 200 ac in Guilford Co on N side of Great Alamance Cr; border: his own deeded land on S, on E by Henry Barnhardt, & on N by Jesse McComb.

1866. Nov. 16, 1779 Robert Rolston enters 100 ac in Guilford Co on Rockhouse Cr on NW side; includes part of improvement where Reubin Gradan lives on upper side and joins John Rukey & Alexander Galbreath.

1867. Nov. 16, 1779 Col. Alexander Martin enters 300 ac in Guilford Co on waters of Jacobs Cr; border: Thomas Allen on S side; includes the Grassy Spring.

page 3
1868. Nov. 17, 1779 Henry Whitesel enters 150 ac in Guilford Co on waters of Allimance and Bever Creeks; border: his own survey, Jacob Scot, & Matthew Swing.
1869. Nov. 17, 1779 Daniel Netherley enters 250 ac in Guilford Co on waters of Reedy fork; border: on N side of his own land; includes improvement called Peter Dillion's field.

1870. Nov. 17, 1779 William Clark enters 200 ac on waters of South Buffaloe Cr in Guilford Co; border: late survey of John & Daniel Gillaspie and John Foster "they being in partnership to one piece of land" and George Barks.

1871. Nov. 17, 1779 William Clark enters 250 ac in Guilford Co on Pole Cat Cr; border: between two lines of late survey of John & Daniel Gillaspie and John Foster "they being in partnership to one peice of land", George Barks, & John Hall.

1872. Nov. 17, 1779 Thomas Donnel enters 125 ac in Guilford Co on waters of S Buffaloe Cr; border: survey of David Kerr on S, John Brown on E, & Donnol on W.

1873. Nov. 17, 1779 David Kerr enters 300 ac in Guilford Co on both sides of S Buffaloe Cr; border: David Kerr's survey on W and Jacob Strickling on N.

page 4
1874. Nov. 17, 1779 Michael Patterson enters 200 ac in Guilford Co between George Ingles, Matthew Russell, William Gilmore, & "my" own entry.

1875. withdrawn 19th. Nov. 17, 1779 Isaiah Watkins enters 200 ac in Guilford Co; border: lower end of his own line, Tate, & Samuel Rogers.

1876. Nov. 17, 1779 Isham Bobbit enters 200 ac on waters of Bever Cr in Guilford Co; border: John Coulton on S and John Moore on E.

1877. Nov. 17, 1779 Charles Bruce enters 100 ac on waters of Blewis Cr in Guilford Co; between "plantation" where Ralph Norris resides and road from Dan R to Salisbury.

1878. Nov. 17, 1779 James Hunter enters 300 ac in Guilford Co; border: his own N line, Archibald Hughes, on E side of Beversland Cr, & on branch of said creek.

1879. Nov. 17, 1779 William Shaw enters 300 ac on waters of Great Allimance Cr in Guilford Co; border: Hugh Shaw and running E.

1880. Nov. 17, 1779 William Kellum enters 200 ac in Guilford Co on S side of Mayo R; border: James Brison on S and Lambath Dodson on N.

page 5
1881. Nov. 17, 1779 James Riggins enters 150 ac in Guilford Co; border: his survey at upper end; includes a small improvement.

1882. Nov. 17, 1779 Almon Grim enters 100 ac in Guilford Co on both sides of Buffaloe Cr; border: John Tate, Drury Hutchison, & John During.

1883. Nov. 17, 1779 William Duff enters 100 ac in Guilford Co on waters of S Buffaloe Cr; between claimint's deeded land, joins Jesse Weatherby, & late survey of John Gillaspie on W.

1884. Nov. 17, 1779 Ralph Gorrel enters 200 ac in Guilford Co on waters of S Buffaloe Cr; border: John McDonnels on E & S and late survey of Gorrel on S.
1885. Nov. 17, 1779 William Bethell enters 200 ac in Guilford Co; between Larken Purpoint, Thomas Mullin, & Natley Jordon.

1886. Nov. 17, 1779 Edward Meglamery enters 200 ac in Guilford Co on Reedy fork; border: "my" late survey and James Barr's deeded land.

1887. Nov. 17, 1779 Bennet Bradford enters 400 ac in Guilford Co on waters of Readox Cr; border: Francis Cummin, John Ballinger's entry, & William Rogers' entry; includes Richard Williams improvement.

1888. Nov. 17, 1779 William King enters 200 ac on Stones fork of Wolf Island Cr; border: Birchfields fork, conditional line made by Mark Lonoon & said King, on N side of ridge near "ridge of Rocks", Poeson fields spring, great fork of Rocky Br, & N fork of said branch.

page 6
1889. Nov. 17, 1779 John Job enters 50 ac on waters of Allamance Cr in Guilford Co; border: on E by deeded land of Peter Low, on N by entry of Matthew R(blank), & W by deeded land of George Engle.

1890. Nov. 17, 1779 Isaac Periman enters 200 ac in Guilford Co on Brushy fork of Jacobs Cr; border: George Carron and said Periman's former entry.

1891. Nov. 18, 1779 Mary Kernochan enters 200 ac in Guilford Co on Long Br of Reedy fork waters of Haw R; border: SE corner of Andrew & John Kernochan entry and E along John White.

1892. Nov. 18, 1779 James Warnick (sic) enters 200 ac in Guilford Co on both sides of Beluis Cr; border: Drury Hutchins on E, John Sutherlin on S, & runs up and down the creek.

1893. Nov. 18, 1779 James Warnock enters 16 ac in Guilford Co on both sides of Bleuis Cr; border: "the county" on W, James Riggins on E, and runs on both sides of creek.

1894. Nov. 18, 1779 Leven Wright enters 80 ac in Guilford Co on waters of Deep R; border: on W side of survey of Thomas Henderson where John Hussy (or Hupy) lives and on E side of survey by John McCoy on tract where Jonathan Maren lives.

1895.   Nov. 18, 1779 Robert Dewing enters 50 ac in Guilford Co on Bever Island Cr; includes an old school house.

1896. Nov. 18, 1779 Robert Corry enters 100 ac in Guilford Co between Haw R and "by" Troublesom Cr; border: John Curry esq, Capt. John Helms, Boyd, & McTeer.

page 7
1897. Nov. 19, 1779 Brumfield Ridley enters 640 ac in Guilford Co on both sides of "the" great branch and Ready fork of Haw R; border: on N Charles Bruce esq; includes two improvements.

1898. Nov. 20, 1779 Robert Gilbreath enters 200 ac in Guilford Co; border: widow Dick's deeded land and David Massey's deeded; includes the improvement where said Robert Gilbreath lives.

1899. caveated by Moses Balinger and William Brittin in part. Nov. 22, 1779 John Nelson enters 200 ac in Guilford Co near Horsepen Cr; border: Joseph Unthanks, William Brittin, & Eleaner Hunt's deeded land; includes improvements of Moses Balinger and William Brittin.

1900. Nov. 23, 1779 Richard Simpson sr enters 150 ac in Guilford Co on Mares fork of Haw R; border: Cain Carrol's NW corner.

1901. Nov. 24, 1779 Nathan Thurp enters 300 ac in Guilford Co on S side of Redy fork; border: Peter King sr's deeded land on E, Joshua Edwards on S, & George Rail on W; includes improvement Steven lives on.

1902. Nov. 25, 1779 James Carruthers enters 400 ac in Guilford Co on branch of Brushey fork of Jacobs Cr and head of Brushey fork; border: Martha Curuthers on N, on S by vacant land, on E by George Castle, & on W by vacant land.

1903. Nov. 27, 1779 John Adkinson enters 100 ac in Guilford Co on branch of Hogans Cr; border: William Williams' entry on W side.

page 8
1904. Nov. 27, 1779 James Henderson enters 100 ac in Guilford Co on branch of Belews Cr; border: James Wright sr "leaving it" on N side and James Wright jr's claim on W; includes a small improvement.

1905. Nov. 27, 1779 William Gamble enters 200 ac in Guilford Co on waters of Great Allamance Cr; between George Coble, which was formerly property of John Fips, Findley Shaw's entry, George Ingles.

1906. Nov. 29, 1779 Robert Shaw and William Shaw enter 400 ac in Guilford Co on waters of Big Allamance Cr; border: N side of Edward Long's improvement and running E; includes Edward Long's improvement.

1907. Nov. 29, 1779 Robert Shaw enters 250 ac in Guilford Co on waters of Big Allamance Cr; border: on S side of John Barkley's improvement; includes John Bartley's improvement.

1908. Nov. 29, 1779 Robert Rankins enters 10 ac in Guilford Co on waters of N Buffellow Cr on S side of said creek; border: on E by Ralph Garrel's survey and on N & W by said Rankins' deeded land.

1909. Nov. 29, 1779 William Jinkins enters 600 ac in Guilford Co on waters of Bobcat Cr; includes improvement of Michael Swim and William Swim.

page 9
1910. Nov. 29, 1779 Andrew Hull enters 250 ac in Guilford Co on waters of Rose Cr of Haw R; border: John Sarratt's corner, Cunningham, Walter Denney (sic), & William Denny; includes "my" own improvement and a rock known as the Flat Rock.

1911. Nov. 30, 1779 Abraham Spencer enters 300 ac in Guilford Co; border: Wm Fruman and on N side of Brushes field fork.

1912. Dec. 4, 1779 Josiah McBride enters 120 ac in Guilford Co on waters of Allamance Cr; border: on E by John Wiley's deeded land and on W by Andrew Findley; includes part of improvement he lives on.

1913. Dec. 4, 1779 William Radford enters 100 ac in Guilford Co on W fork of Rockey Br; border: Ralph Norris' claim up both sides of branch.

1914. caveated by Drury Hutchins; caveat withdrawn. Dec. 4, 1779 Ralph Norris enters 150 ac in Guilford Co on Rockey Br; border: Drury Hutchins.

1915. Dec. 6, 1779 William Hindman enters 100 ac in Guilford Co on waters of Redy fork; border: a branch on S side of WIlliam Rueses land and Mr Frohock.

page 10
1916. Dec. 6, 1779 Thadeus Beall enters 400 ac in Guilford Co on both sides of S Buffellow Cr; border: a claim where John Haskins lives purchased from Bennet Bradford; includes improvement where Thomas Green lived and place widow Short lived on when she married Thomas Green.

1917. Dec. 16, 1779 Nathan Shelley enters 250 ac on Guilford Co; between William Gray, George Leasure Brown, & John Hamilton.

1918. Dec. 6, 1779 Richard Lewis enters 250 ac in Guilford Co on both sides of Lick Br waters of Haw R on S side; border: W of Abraham Endsley.

1919. Dec. 6, 1779 John Joyce (or Joice) enters 400 ac in Guilford Co on waters of Mayo R; border: on N side of Rick Perron Cardwell.

1920. Dec. 6, 1779 Nathan Peeples enters 300 ac in Guilford Co on waters of Jacobs Cr; border: on S side of David Peeples' land he purchased of John Nix and vacant land.

1921. Dec. 6, 1779 Richard Lewis enters 200 ac in Guilford Co on Bever Cr and Lick Br; border: Andrew Endsley and Robert Blakeny's old claim.

1922. Dec. 6, 1779 Thomas Clark enters 300 ac in Guilford Co on S side of S Buffallow Cr; border: Jacob Stricklin sr on S & W and runs down Buffallow Cr near Alexander Gray's improvement.

1923. Dec. 6, 1779 William Bethell enters 200 ac in Guilford Co; on both sides of the big road called Ironworks Road between Larkin Peirpont's entry, Peter Lewis, & widow Fletther and joins Saml Wats deeded land.

page 11
1924. Dec. 6, 1779 Robert Peasley enters 50 ac in Guilford Co on waters of Rock Cr; border: his own corner and John Smith.

1925. Dec. 7, 1779 William Reed enters 250 ac in Guilford Co on waters of Redy fork; border: Charles Bruce on N; includes "plantation" where John Harry lives.

1926. Dec. 7, 1779 William Reed enters 200 ac in Guilford Co on waters of Redy fork; border: Benjamin Brittin on N; includes improvement where Charles Canady lives.

1927. Dec. 7, 1779 John Rankin enters 75 ac in Guilford Co on N side of Buffalow Cr; border: James Donnel's SE corner, Robert Smith, & Rankin.

1928. Dec. 7, 1779 John Rusing enters 200 ac in Guilford Co on waters of Hickory Cr of Mayo R; border: James Jackson on S and Charles Gibson on E.

1929. Dec. 7, 1779 John Whitsel enters 200 ac in Guilford Co on waters of Buckhorn Cr; border: Adam Apple and William Nelson.

1930. Dec. 7, 1779 Henry Whitsel enters 100 ac in Guilford Co on Rockey Cr; border: Davis Lour (or Love) and Jacob Howel.
1931. Dec. 7, 1779 Jacob Grunway enters 500 ac in Guilford Co on Aarons Cr; border: John Smith's deeded land below the school house, Robert Peasley, & "his" corner.

1932. Dec. 8, 1779 William Jackson enters 120 ac in Guilford Co on head waters of Hays Br waters of Redy fork of Haw R; border: Love's corner and his own corner.

1933. Dec. 9, 1779 James Jackson enters 300 ac in Guilford Co on waters of Hicory Cr; border: the county line.

1934. Dec. 9, 1779 Joel Gibson enters 170 ac in Guilford Co on waters of Green Spring; border: his own land and Andrew Gibson.

page 12
1935. Dec. 10, 1779 David Kerr enters 300 ac in Guilford Co on waters of Allamance Cr; border: entry of Joseph Kenedy, widow Jinkins, and a late survey of William Brigance; includes improvement William Brigance lately lived on.

1936. Dec. 10, 1779 Adam Lowman enters 290 ac in Guilford Co on waters of Redy fork; border: widow Flack, John Goodner (or Gosdner), William Smith, & his own improvement.

1937. Dec. 11, 1779 Joel Sanders enters 300 ac in Guilford Co on N side of N fork of Deep R; border: deeded land of Joel Sanders and a former entry of William Dent jr; includes two improvements.

1938. Dec. 10, 1779 Andrew Findley jr enters 200 ac on waters of Great Allamance Cr in Guilford Co; border: Findley Shaw's corner.

1939. Dec. 11, 1779 Samuel Fraser (or Frazer) enters 350 ac in Guilford Co on waters of Bull Run; border: entry of Valentine Allen; includes improvement of Thomas Pierce.

1940. Dec. 11, 1779 John Haley enters 350 ac in Guilford Co on N side of S fork of Deep R; border: meeting house land; includes John Wall and William Beard's improvement.

1941. Dec. 11, 1779 William Clark enters 350 ac in Guilford Co on both sides of Pole cat Cr; border: deeded land of Peter Dick; includes John Stones improvement.

1942. Dec. 11, 1779 William Clark enters 300 ac in Guilford Co on branch of Cedar Cr waters of Allamance Cr; border: a claim of Lewis Iseley on E; includes claim John Boon lives on "it being an old entry".

1943. Dec. 11, 1779 Daniel Brittin enters 265 ac in Guilford Co on waters of Brush Cr; border: Aaron Mendinghall, John Clark's deeded land, & Robert Gilbreath's conditional line.

page 13
1944. Dec. 11, 1779 George Parks enters 50 ac in Guilford Co on waters of N Buffallow Cr; border: his former lines and Bennet Bradford.

1945. Dec. 20, 1779 George Coble enters 200 ac in Guilford Co on waters of Little Allamance Cr; border: deeded land he lives on, John Philip Clap's land he purchased from Daniel England, & a tract of McCullock; includes a small improvement of said Coble.

1946. Dec. 25, 1779 James Campbell enters 400 ac in Guilford Co on Lick fork of Hogans Cr; border: widow Savage's corner, Jacob Williams, & John Hancock; includes improvement where Daniel McCloud and Overby lives.
1947. Dec. 25, 1779 James Campbell enters 400 ac in Guilford Co on waters of Deep R; border: John McCoy and William Beard; includes improvement where John Wall lives.

1948. Dec. 27, 1779 William Overbay enters 100 ac in Guilford Co on waters of Lick fork; border: John Smith and Ironworks road; includes William Sprus improvement.

1949. Dec. 27, 1779 Alexander Caldwell enters 400 ac in Guilford Cr; border: Robert Blackley's NE corner and vacant land.

1950. caveated by Nathan Dillin Mar. 16, 1780; caveat ruled good order of court. Dec. 27, 1779 Alexander Caldwell entered 200 ac in Guilford Co on waters of Bever Cr; border: William Starbuck, Blakley's entry, & Nathan Dillin's entry.

1951. Dec. 27, 1779 Moses Craner enters 150 ac in Guilford Co on waters of S Buffallow Cr; border: his own land, Samuel Sulivant, Thomas Mager, James Frazer, & Patrick Mullen.

page 14
1952. Dec. 28, 1779 James Hamilton enters 300 ac in Guilford Co on waters of Great Allamance Cr; border: Christian Iseley.

1953. Dec. 29, 1779 Nathan Dillin enters 200 ac in Guilford Co on Redy fork; border: on S side of Daniel Dillin's Bever Cr deeded land and claimant's own survey on Redy fork; includes part of an improvement.

1954. Dec. 31, 1779 Joshua Dean enters 200 ac in Guilford Co on waters of Haw R; border: two entrys made by John Chilint.

1955. Jan. 1, 1780 James Sarratt enters 100 ac in Guilford Co on waters of Roses Cr; border: on E side of his own deeded land and on S of Cunningham's deeded land; "no improvement".

1956. Jan. 1, 1780 John Sarratt and Andrew Hall enters 400 ac in Guilford Co on heads of Chesnut Cr and Giles Cr waters of Haw R; border: on W by Cunningham's deeded land and late entry of James Sarratt, on N by late survey of John McKibbins, & on E by Rev James Campbell's survey.

1957. Jan. 1, 1780 Bennet Bradford enters 50 ac in Guilford Co on fork of Deep R; border: a former survey of said Bradford.

1958. Jan. 1, 1780 Nathan Dillin enters 400 ac in Guilford Co on waters of Redy fork; border: Robert Blackley's E corner on Hockey Br and Daniel Dillin's deeded land; includes his own improvement.

page 15
1959. Jan. 1, 1780 Thaddens Beall enters 640 ac in Guilford Co on Bull Run; border: James Martin and his own entry; includes John & Paul Macy's improvement.

1960. Jan. 1, 1780 Charles Galloway enters 640 ac in Guilford Co on waters of Dan R; border: back line of his deeded land where he lives.

1961. Jan. 1, 1780 Constantine Perkins enters 640 ac in Guilford Co on waters of Clarks Cr; border: (blank) line; includes Jesse Hammond's improvement.

1962. Jan. 3, 1780 Robert Small enters 200 ac in Guilford Co on branch of Rockhouse Cr; border: James (blank), Mr (or Mc) Hoggard, & entry of John Guess where "he" now lives.

1963. Jan. 3, 1780 Robert Small enters (blank) ac in Guilford Co on Great Troublesom Cr; border: Hugh (blank), William Plumbley, & his own land.

1964. Jan. 3, 1780 Robert Small enters 100 ac in Guilford Cr on both sides of Gleady Br branch of Great Troublesom Cr; border: "Aunders to Lane".

1965. Jan. 8, 1780 John Lashley enters 50 ac in Guilford Co on waters of Brush Cr; border: Aaron Mendinghall's deeded land, Richard Howard's deeded land, & Daniel Brittain's entry.

1966. Jan. 14, 1780 Sarah Allison enters 300 ac in Guilford Co on both sides of Beaver Cr; includes Dillons mill.

page 16
1967. Jan. 18, 1780 William Way enters 400 ac in Guilford Co on both sides of Hickory Cr; border: entry of Bennet Bradford, William Rodgers' entry, & Robert Irwin's entry; includes "James Anthony and William Mays".

1968. Jan. 18, 1780 David Hamilton enters 200 ac in Guilford Co; border: E corner of his own land, head of springs of Poson [fork ?], & joins head springs of (blank).

1969. Jan. 18, 1780 George Parks enters 400 ac in Guilford Co on Ceder Cr waters of Great Allamance Cr; border: deeded land of Lodowick and Iseley; includes improvements where John Boon lives.

1970. Jan. 18, 1780 James Wilson and William Jackson enters 250 ac in Guilford Co on Rock Br; border: Samuel Fulton's line Northward.

1971. Jan. 19, 1780 Jerrett Branden enters 100 ac in Guilford Co on waters of Wolf Island Cr; border: his line on S and William Young on N.

1972. Jan. 19, 1780 William Young enters 200 ac in Guilford Co on Wolf Island Cr; border: on S side of late entry of Jennett (sic) Branden.

1973. Jan. 19, 1780 Charles Hanes enters 150 ac in Guilford Cr on waters of Wolf Island Cr; border: on N side of his own land.

page 17
1974. Jan. 19, 1780 Joseph Chassir enters 150 ac in Guilford Co on waters of big Allamance Cr; border: on E corner of "said" Morrow's land.

1975. Jan. 24, 1780 Risdon Moore enters 120 ac in Guilford Co on waters of Deep R; border: deeded land of Elijah Mendinall on W, deeded land of George Slatkas on E, & John Goldens on S; includes small improvement of George Slatkis.

1976. Jan. 24, 1780 Stephen Sanders enters 200 ac in Guilford Co on waters of Deep R; border: deeded land of Sanders on N and William Gardner; includes small improvement where Elijah Stanley did lives.

1977. caveated by John Haley; entry withdrawn. Jan. 24, 1780 Elijah Charles enters 200 ac in Guilford Co on waters of Deep R; border: a survey of John Healey, claims of Tullerton Johnson, & entry of Thos Busey.

1978. Jan. 25, 1780 James Barr enters 100 ac in Guilford Co on waters of Reedy fork; border: his own corner and William Scott's late survey.

1979. Jan. 25, 1780 Andrew Scott [enters] 100 ac on waters of Little Troublesome Cr in Guilford Co; border: Robert Barr on N & Hugh Hanes on S.

1980. Jan. 28, 1780 William Obannon enters 150 ac in Guilford Co on Thachers Br of Hogans Cr; border: Thomas Hanes' deeded line; includes improvement where he lives.

page 18
1981. Jan. 31, 1780 Nathan Dillin enters 80 ac in Guilford Co on Redy fork of Haw R; border: William Starbuck's NE corner of "his" deeded land, Caldwell's entry, Daniel Dillin's deeded land, & vacant land.

1982. Feb. 1, 1788 William Dent enters 108 ac in Guilford Co on waters of Richland Cr; border: on W by said Dent's entry, on E by survey of William Dick, & entry of David Morrow; "before one" W Gowdy.

1983. withdrawn. Feb. 1, 1780 William Dent enters 100 ac in Guilford Co on Horsepin Br on Redy fork; border: on N by deeded land bought by siad Dent from William Foster, on W by Macey's deeded land, on E by entry of said Dent, & on S by land where Isaac White did live; entered before "one" W Gowdy.

1984. withdrawn & money returned 9£ 10s. Feb. 1, 1780 Nathan Dillon enters 300 ac in Guilford Co on Moons Cr; border: on N side of his entry where Joseph Perkins lives.

1985. Feb. 1, 1780 Hugh Copelin enters 250 ac in Guilford Co on waters of big Allamance Cr; border: on E side of Samuel Deveny, on W of John Copelin's deeded land, on S of Robert Fields, on N of Edward Long, & on both sides of Speaker's road.

1986. Feb. 3, 1780 John & Daniel Gillespie and John Foster enter 200 ac in Guilford Co on waters of Pole catt Cr; border: on N by their own (written over John Hall) survey and on S by survey of George Parks.

page 19
1987. Feb. 3, 1780 John & Daniel Gillespie and John Foster enter 200 ac in Guilford Co; border: on W by survey of James Frazer, on N by survey of John Hall, & on S by their own survey; includes an improvement.

1988. Feb. 3, 1780 William Allen enters 100 ac in Guilford Co on waters of Hogans Cr; border: Peter ONeal and John & Joshua Allin's entry.

1989. Feb. 3, 1780 John Mattock enters 640 ac in Guilford Co on waters of Brushy fork; border: on E side of William Allin's entry and N side of Samuel (blank) entry; includes his improvement made by Joseph Owen.

1990. Feb. 3, 1780 William Jones enters 150 ac on Brushy fork on Great Rockhouse Cr in Guilford Co; border: on W side of his former entry.

1991. Feb. 3, 1780 Job Barber enters 100 ac in Guilford Co on Brushy fork of Great Rockhouse Cr; border: S of John Baker's entry.

1992. Feb. 4, 1780 Charles Baker enters 150 ac in Guilford Co on Brushey fork of Piney Cr; border: on N side of his former entry.

1993. Feb. 4, 1780 Charles Baker enters 300 ac in Guilford Co on Brushey fork of Piney Cr on both sides of said creek; border: claims of John Gruss (or Guess); whereon his now lives.

1994. Feb. 4, 1780 Alexander Lyall enters 100 ac on Maho R in Guilford Co; border: below David Hanbey's ford and vacant land.

page 20
1995. Feb. 8, 1780 Nathan Thacker enters 200 ac in Guilford Co on waters of Pruit's (or Pauit's) fork of Hogans Cr; border: Zachariah Thacker and on W side of widow Hanes.

1996. Feb. 14, 1780 Robert Moor enters 500 ac in Guilford Co on branch of Balue's Cr; border: on S of John Moor and John Whitesides.

1997. Feb. 18, 1780 Thomas Grogan enters 100 ac in Guilford Co on W branch of Double Cr; border: on E side of his own entry and on W of Benjamin (blank) claim.

1998. Feb. 18, 1780 Joseph Stanley enters 100 ac in Guilford Co on branches of Reedy fork; border: on E side of his own land.

1999. Feb. 18, 1780 Moses Stawhon enters 100 ac in Guilford on Cabbin Br of Reedy fork of Haw R; border: his own land on W side.

2000. Feb. 18, 1780 James Carruthers enters 400 ac in Guilford Co on branch of Brushy fork of Jacobs Cr; border: on S of Martha Caruthers and on N, E & W of vacant land.

2001. Feb. 18, 1780 Aaron Arnold enters 200 ac in Guilford Co on waters of Lick fork of Hogans Cr; border: entry of Zachariah Savage, William Speres, & David McCloud on E.

2002. Feb. 19, 1780 James Moor enters 250 ac in Guilford at head of Reedy Cr; includes improvement formerly Richard Tayler's; border: Cornelius Cook and on E of Robert Moor.

page 21
2003. Feb. 19, 1780 William Miller enters 50 ac in Guilford Co on waters of big Rockhouse Cr; border: Benjamin Hoggard's corner, Francis Saundors, & William Miller.

2004. Feb. 21, 1780 Charles Bruce esq enters 150 ac in Guilford Co on waters of Haw R; border: Malachi Reeves on W and Henry Works on S.

2005. Feb. 21, 1780 William Hough enters 250 ac in Guilford Co on waters of Deep R; border: NW corner of Leven Charles' survey.

2006. Feb. 21, 1780 John (blank) enters 125 ac in Guilford Co; border: the county line, on S by Jno (blank), & on W by Henry (blank).

2007. Feb. 21, 1780 Alexander Caldwell esq enters 200 ac in Guilford Co; border: E & W line of Robert Blackley's entry #1609 on N side and vacant land.

2008. Feb. 21, 1780 Thomas Garner enters 240 ac in Guilford Co on Haw R; border: Brigel Browner on N and Philip Rodes on W.

2009. Feb. 21, 1780 John Harper enters 80 ac in Guilford Co on Reedy fork; border: George Larance on W & S and county line on E; "with" the improvement.

2010. Feb. 21, 1780 Finley Stuart enters 100 ac in Guilford Co on waters of Great Allamance Cr; border: John Tom's corner, William Eaking, Robt Allison, his own land, & Henry Eustis McCullock.

page 22
2011. Feb. 21, 1780 James Saunders enters 150 ac in Guilford Co; border: Matthias Mount on N side; includes the Rocky Br.

2012. Feb. 21, 1780 James Saunders enters 100 ac in Guilford Co; border: Abraham Philips on E, his own late entry, & William Miller.

2013. Feb. 21, 1780 James Wright enters 300 ac in Guilford on Tass Cr a branch of Bleus's Cr; includes two small improvements.

2014. Feb. 21, 1780 James Saunders enters 320 ac in Guilford Co on waters of Rockhouse Cr; border: on S side "on" John Prvitte land, Matthew Mount, & Benjamin Hoggard.

2015. Feb. 21, 1780 William Williams and James Wright enters 100 ac in Guilford Co; border: county line, James Wright's entry and William Kinman's entry in Surry Co.

2016. Feb. 22, 1780 Henry Barnhardt enters 200 ac in Guilford Co on waters of Allamance Cr; border: his own entry on W, Adam Starr on S, Adam Lawrance on S side, & David "clow" on E.

2017. Feb. 22, 1780 William Morgan enters 200 ac in Guilford Co on waters of Stinking Quarter Cr; border: on W by James ONeal.

2018. Feb. 22, 1780 William Kellum enters 100 ac in Guilford Co; border: the county line, Lambert Dottson (or Dollson) on W and Zachariah King on S.

2019. Feb. 22, 1780 Francis Maxwel enters 200 ac in Guilford Co on Lawrences Cr; border: Andrew Law and William Montgomery.

page 23
2020. Feb. 22, 1780 Charles Bruce enters 250 ac in Guilford Co on both sides of S fork of upper Hogans Cr; border: Samuel Finley and Margery Feagan.

2021. Feb. 22, 1780 Charles Bruce enters 40 ac on waters of Reedy fork of Haw R on both sides Bruce's road on Guilford Co; border: Nathan Peeples on N, claiment's own land on E & S, and David Peeples on W.

2022. Feb. 22, 1780 Samuel Finley enters 200 ac in Guilford Co on Williams Br of upper Hogans Cr; border: on N by William Williams and John Adkinson.

2023. Feb. 22, 1780 Samuel Finley enters 150 ac on Tapps Cr in Guilford Co; border: James Wright's entry on W.

2024. Feb. 22, 1780 William Steplow enters 150 ac in Guilford Co on Ragged Br; border: "the fork" and Joseph Odle.

2025. Feb. 22, 1780 David Hamilton enters 150 ac in Guilford Co on head of Little Buffaloe Cr; border: John Roch.
2026. Feb. 22, 1780 William Bostick enters 300 ac in Guilford Co on both sides of Reeds Cr waters of Beluis Cr; includes Colson's cabbin.

2027. Feb. 22, 1780 James ONeal enters 640 ac in Guilford Co on Stinking Quarter Cr; border: entry of William Dent on W, Frances Linsbery on E, & Philip Show on N.

2028. Feb. 22, 1780 George Pierce enters 400 ac in Guilford Co on waters of Blewis Cr; border: Surry county line; near head of Rocky Br.

2029. Feb. 22, 1780 Charles Lewel enters 100 ac in Guilford Co; border: Crunck and Curtis.

2030. Feb. 22, 1780 Thomas Hays enters 150 ac in Guilford Co; border: on W side of widow Nelson and Joseph Taylor on waters of Haw R.

page 24
2031. Feb. 22, 1780 Andrew Wilson enters 400 ac in Guilford Co on N side of Haw R; border: N of his deeded land, E of widow Dilworth's deeded land, & W of William Wilson's late entry.

2032. Feb. 23, 1780 William Plumley enters 640 ac in Guilford Co on Piney Cr waters of Troublesom Cr; border: on E corner of Ironworks land, widow Dixon's N line, & Robert Brooks; includes improvement purchased from William Fowler.

2033. Feb. 23, 1780 Cornelius Cook enters 100 ac on Wrights fork of Balews Cr in Guilford Co; border: on W of Nathaniel Fadberry's entry.

2034. Feb. 23, 1780 Jeremiah Porton enters 200 ac on waters of Haw R in Guilford Co; border: his own entry brought from Brsel Browner; "all woodland".

2035. Feb. 23, 1780 William Brown enters 100 ac on (blank) of Deep R and Reedy fork in Guilford Co; border: William Gray and Benjamin Hairgroves; includes his own improvement.

2036. Feb. 23, 1780 Abraham Philips enters 100 ac in Guilford Co; border: his former entry on W, William Jones on E, & James Sanders on S.

2037. Feb. 23, 1780 Abraham Philips enters 75 ac in Guilford Co on Wolf Island Cr; border: James Wardlaw on W, Nathaniel Harrison on E, & John McConill (or McCarrill).

2038. Feb. 23, 1780 Isaac Philip enters 200 ac in Guilford Co on Slippery Rock Br of Great Rockhouse Cr; border or near: Thomas Loyd's N line.

page 25

2039. Feb. 23, 1780 John McCarrel jr enters 50 ac in Guilford Co on both sides of S fork of Piney Br; border: on N "on" John McKee and on W by John Pimble.

2040. Feb. 23, 1780 Reuben Cook enters 600 ac in Guilford Co on Matrimony Cr; border: Samuel Gates lower line and the county line.

2041. Feb. 23, 1780 William Akin enters 50 ac in Guilford Co between waters of Bear Cr and big Allamance Cr; border: on N side claimant's "plantation".

2042. Feb. 23, 1780 John Harford Taylor enters 400 ac in Guilford Co on waters of Lick fork; border: Jacob Williams corner and Spere's dividing line.

2043. Feb. 23, 1780 David Little enters 100 ac in Guilford Co on waters of Hogans Cr; between Samuel Watt and William Settle.

2044. Feb. 23, 1780 William Dent enters 400 ac in Guilford Co on waters of Allamance Cr; border: deeded land of Lodwick Iseley; includes improvement by Christian and Lodowick Iseley.

2045. Feb. 24, 1780 Christian Fall enters 200 ac in Guilford Co on waters of Haw R; includes improvement where Jacob Devalt lives.

2046. Feb. 24, 1780 Capt Arthur Falls enters 300 ac in Guilford Co on waters of Haw R; includes improvement of Christian Falls.

2047. Feb. 24, 1780 Capt Arthur Falls enters 22 ac in Guilford Co on waters of Allamance Cr; border: on E side of his land.

page 26

2048. Feb. 24, 1780 Matthew Russel enters 280 ac in Guilford Co on waters of Great Allamance; border: on E by entry of Jacob Job, on S by Christian Foud, & a former entry of said Russel.

2049. Feb. 24, 1780 Robert Martin enters 150 ac in Guilford Co on SE fork of Jacobs Cr; between Francis Young and Adam Baker.

2050. Feb. 24, 1780 Drury Hutchens enters 100 ac in Guilford Co on waters of Kerbeys Cr; border: Isaac Whitworth and Ralph Norris.

2051. Feb. 24, 1780 Joshua Maberry enters 200 ac in Guilford Co on waters of Falls Cr and Paupau Cr; border: Virginia line at Hay's corner.

2052. Feb. 24, 1780 James Joyce enters 200 ac in Guilford Co on N side of Dan R on Lick fork a branch of Buffellow Island Cr.

2053. Feb. 24, 1780 Drury Watson enters 350 ac in Guilford Co on both sides of Redy fork (write over) of Haw R; border: Surry county line.

2054. Feb. 25, 1780 William Clark jr enters 250 ac in Guilford Co on waters of Hogans Cr; border: Daniel Allen.

2055. Feb. 25, 1780 Gidion Johnson enters 250 ac in Guilford Co on N side of Dan R; border: George Peay and William Covington.

2056. Feb. 25, 1780 Drury Hutchings enters 50 ac in Guilford Co two fish sholes on Dan R; between John Dearing and widow Hoggatt.

2057. Feb. 25, 1780 Edward Stubblefield enters 200 ac in Guilford Co on W side of Wolf Island Cr; border: Capt Browder and vacant land; includes "plantation" where he lives.

2058. Feb. 29, 1780 Drury Smith enters 150 ac in Guilford Co on waters of Pawpaw Cr; border: Smith, Grogan's corner, & Dotton.
page 27
2059. Feb. 29, 1780 Benjamin Gowing enters 200 ac in Guilford Co on Double Cr; border: James Joice and Thomas Grogan.

2060. Feb. 29, 1780 Charles Baker enters 200 ac in Guilford Co on waters of Jacobs Cr; border: on SE side of his own survey, on N side of Thomas Massey, & on W side of Thomas Brown.

2061. Feb. 29, 1780 James Williams enters 100 ac in Guilford Co on S side of Hogans Cr; border: Peter Oneal's N corner and said Williams' corner.

2062. Feb. 29, 1780 Ely Newland enters 320 ac in Guilford Co on waters of Stinkin Quarter Cr; border: Samuel Law, William Plunket, Thomas McCullock, & Orange County line.

2063. Feb. 29, 1780 John Thomas enters 100 ac in Guilford Co on Meadow Br of Brushy fork of Jacobs Cr.

2064. Feb. 29, 1780 John McKibbin enters 100 ac in Guilford Co; border: on E side of his former entry, on N side of McCambler, & Meter's old line.

2065. Feb. 29, 1780 John McPeak enters 150 ac in Guilford Co on waters of upper Hogans Cr; border: Michael Thomas' corner and Benjamin Powen.

2066. Feb. 29, 1780 Hugh Linch enters 100 ac in Guilford Co on N side of big Troublesome Cr.

2067. Mar. 1, 1780 John Simmons enters 100 ac in Guilford Co on both sides of Piney fork; border: Samuel Denton on N.

2068. Mar. 2, 1780 James Hays enters 300 ac in Guilford Co on N waters of Deep R; border: his old entry on E and S.

page 28
2069. withdrawn Mar. 2, 1780 Samuel Johnson enters 100 ac in Guilford Co; border: on NW "square" of John Coulter's survey, county line on a branch(?) of Blews Cr.

2070. Mar. 3, 1780 Joseph Bell Beall (or Joseph Bell--in index of book) enters 100 ac in Guilford Co on waters of Hicory Cr; border: Bennet Bradford on S.

2071. Mar. 3, 1780 Benjamin Bowen enters 640 ac in Guilford Co on W fork of Hogans Cr; border: on E by Thomas Bowen.

2072. Mar. 3, 1780 Boston Garginger enters 100 ac in Guilford Co on waters of Abots Cr; border: George Waggoner and George Summerman.

2073. Mar. 9, 1780 William Briges (or Bridges) enters 150 ac in waters of N and S Buffellow Cr; border: Samuel Lackey's S line, William Briges, Samuel Patton, & his own line.

2074. Mar. 10, 1780 Nathan Dillin enters 250 ac in Guilford Co on Brush Cr; border: SW corner of his survey where Joseph Pirkins lives.

2075. Mar. 10, 1780 Abraham Philips enters 100 ac in Guilford Cr on Pruits fork of Hogans Cr; border: Joseph Man's NE corner, Thompson Harris, & Vaughan's deeded land.
2076. Mar. 10, 1780 John Johnston enters 200 ac in Guilford Co on waters of Jacobs Cr; border: on E side of Adam Baker.

2077. Mar. 10, 1780 John Johnson enters 300 ac in Guilford Co on waters of Jacobs Cr; border: on W side of Adam Baker.

2078. Mar. 10, 1780 John Holiday (or Holaday) enters 250 ac in Guilford Co; border: Calhoon and John Fleming's survey on Troublesome Cr.

2080. withdrawn. Mar. 10, 1780 Robert Morrow enters 200 ac in Guilford Co on waters of Allamance Cr; "to take up where it may be left out" by James Setts survey of 400 ac; border: Jacob Summers, James Allison, Findley Stewart, Hugh Shaw, Saml Shaw, & John McClean.

2081. Mar. 10, 1780 William Plunkit enters 100 ac in Guilford Co on waters of Stinking Quarter Cr; border: on NW by land where said Plunkitt & Philip Sellers now live and joins Thomas McCulloch's deeded line.

2082. Mar. 10, 1780 John Young enters 500 ac in Guilford Co on Great Rockhouse Cr; border: on S of Abraham Philips' entry, Richard Henderson's entry, & Daniel Obrian's entry.

2083. Mar. 10, 1780 Samuel Rose enters 150 ac in Guilford Co on Piney fork on waters of Dan R.

2084. Mar. 10, 1780 Samuel Short enters 150 ac in Guilford Co; border: Peter Mitchel's N and S line on E side.

2085. Mar. 10, 1780 James Bryon enters 200 ac in Guilford Co on waters of Mayo R; border: N side of his own line and "the" former survey.

2086. Mar. 10, 1780 Zachariah Roberson enters 100 ac in Guilford Co on Hazel Br of Great Rockhouse Cr.

2087. Mar. 10, 1780 James Richey enters 50 ac in Guilford Co on W side of Rockhouse Cr.

2088. Mar. 10, 1780 William Bethel enters 200 ac in Guilford Co on waters of Lick fork Cr between Hogans Cr and Wolf Island Cr; border: Isaac Dorres.

page 30
2089. Mar. 11, 1780 Robert Small enters 350 ac in Guilford Co on both sides of Brushy Br of Piney fork; border: his former entry on E & S, William Miller's conditional line on W; includes an improvement where John Guess lives.

2090. Mar. 11, 1780 Samuel Gates enters 200 ac in Guilford Co on waters of Matrimony Cr of Dan R; border: on N by Virginia line and on W of his own line; includes his improvement.

2091. Mar. 11, 1780 Nicholas Gift enters 100 ac in Guilford Co on waters of Rock Cr; border: his own former entry, Henry Cob's entry, & Garnet Struker's entry "to the North".

2092. Mar. 11, 1780 James Regan enters 200 ac in Guilford Co on waters of Belews Cr; border: his former survey.

2093. Mar. 11, 1780 Thomas Thornburg jr enters 200 ac in Guilford Co on waters of Brush Cr; border: James McGrady, Thomas Thornburg, & Richd Harver.

2094. Mar. 11, 1780 James Fitzgerald enters 520 ac in Guilford Co; border: James Strong, Darby Calaham, & Henery Seales.

2095. Mar. 15, 1780 Isham Browder enters 250 ac in Guilford Co; border: William Farnot, near branch of Wolf Island Cr, "where Browder's line crosses the road", & vacant land.

2096. Mar. 15, 1780 Isham Browder enters 200 ac in Guilford Co; border: Smith, near "his" corner on S side of Wolf Island Cr, & vacant land.

2097. Mar. 16, 1780 Jerimiah Poston enters 100 ac in Guilford Co; border: his own entry "bought of Thomas Reddin" and Isaac Dinnis.

2098. Mar. 16, 1780 Robert Dewing enters 2 ac in Guilford Co on Dann R; border: an island.

page 31
2099. Mar. 17, 1780 William Dickey enters 100 ac in Guilford Co on waters of Allimance; border: William Dickey's N corner and Robeart Nelley.

2100. Mar. 20, 1780 Robert Neeley (or Nealey) enters 200 ac in Guilford Co; border: James Neeley's S corner and Joseph Dobson.

2101. Mar. 20, 1780 George King enters 400 ac in Guilford Co on S side of N fork of Deep R; border: John Sanders deeded land and John McCoy's late entry; includes an improvement.

2102. Mar. 20, 1780 Rees Porter enters 80 ac on Guilford Co on S side of Buffellow Cr below the forks; border: on E by William Montgomery and on W by Alexander Gree.

2103. Mar. 20, 1780 David Linvill enters 300 ac in Guilford Co on W fork of Hogans Cr; border: on S side of Sotetherland (sic) and on both sides of said creek; includes Linvell's improvement.

2104. Mar. 21, 1780 John Pirkle enters 120 ac in Guilford Co on Piney Cr waters; border: on E by John McCurrel, on N by John Bell, & on W by land of said Pirkle.

2105. Mar. 21, 1780 Michael Henderson enters 80 ac in Guilford Co on W fork of upper Hogans Cr; border: Williams survey on S & W; includes on S part of an improvement and wood land on W.

2106. Mar. 21, 1780 Isham Browder enters 200 ac in Guilford Co on N side of Wolf Island Cr; border: his own [land] and Bankston.

2107. Mar. 21, 1780 Archer Blantons Henderson enters 150 ac in Guilford Co on upper Hogans Cr; border: Henderson on N, Sutherland's survey on S, & Linvil's on E side.

2108. Mart. 21, 1780 John McCarrel enters 200 ac in Guilford Co on both sides of Bare Br of Great Rockhouse Cr.

2109. Mar. 21, 1780 William Swaim enters 640 ac in Guilford Co on waters of Poal cat Cr; border: widow Hocket on S; includes three improvements.

page 32
2110. Mar. 22, 1780 Caleb Blegg enters 175 ac in Guilford Co on S side of Deep R; border: Isaac Houlton and conditional line marked "IH" on one side and "IE" on other side.

2111. Mar. 22, 1780 Wirkfield Shropshere enters 100 ac in Guilford Co on White Oak fork of Buffellow Cr; border: his former entry of 100 ac.
2112. Mar. 23, 1780 William Lomax enters 200 ac in Guilford Co on Brush Cr; border: S corner of Rankin's deeded land, John Unthanks, & Abel Night; includes "the" improvement.

2113. Mar. 24, 1780 Robert Adams enters 200 ac in Guilford Co on waters of Allemance Cr and a branch called Red Water; border: entry of Matthew Hamilton and James Hunter; includes improvement where he lives.

2114. Mar. 24, 1780 William Barnett enters 200 ac in Guilford Co on waters of Stinkin Quarter Cr; border: on E side of his former entry.

2115. Mar. 25, 1780 Thomas Hamilton enters 140 ac in Guilford Co of waters of (Stinkin Quarter--lined out) big Allemance Cr; border: John Smith's claim "on the (blank) of said Smith's claim".

2116. Mar. 25, 1780 George Stewart enters 200 ac in Guilford Co on waters of Rock Cr; border: Robert Peasley on N.

2117. Mar. 27, 1780 William Shaw enters 200 ac in Guilford Co on waters of Horspen Cr; border: entry made by Michal on E, William Brittin's on W, & Thomas Thornbury on S.

2118. Mar. 28, 1780 Francis Young enters 200 ac in Guilford Co; border: W end of his own new entry, S of John Nelson's new entry, & runs up the Long Br.

2119. Mar. 28, 1780 William Dent enters 100 ac in Guilford Co on waters of Stinking Quarter Cr; border: on E & N lines of survey of "the" Dents and E by entry of Thaddeus Beal.

page 33
2120. Mar. 28, 1780 Charles Bruce enters 95 ac on waters of Hogans Cr in Guilford Co; border: his own [land] and Patrick Burns (& Hezekiah Gates--lined out).

2121. Mar. 28, 1780 Charles Bruce enters 100 ac in Guilford Co on waters of Hogans Cr; border: his own [land], Patrick Burns, & Hezekiah Gates.

2122. Mar. 28, 1780 Arthur Carney enters 150 ac in Guilford Co on both sides of Richland Cr; [border:] James Green on E, John Wolfington on S, widow Cursey on W, William Lain on N, & a branch.

2123. Mar. 29, 1780 Robert Rolston enters 200 ac in Guilford Co on waters of Jacobs Cr; border: entry made by Alexr Martin esq on N and entry of Saml Martin on S; includes part of Court house road.

2124. Apr. 1, 1780 Edward Holland enters 60 ac in Guilford Co; border: his own land on S, Francis Wright on E, & James McCuistiong on N & W.

2125. Apr. 1, 1780 James Coots enters 50 in Guilford Co; border: on S side of his own land on Redy fork.

2126. Apr. 1, 1780 James Brown enters 200 ac in Guilford Co on N side of Redy fork; [border:] Jeremiah McFadyens desc's W & N lines, Samuel Smith, & John Maxwell; includes the waggon road.

2127. Apra. 1, 1780 John McBride enters 400 ac in Guilford Co on waters of Deep R on S side of N fork of said river; border: Hezekiah Sanders; includes improvement John Sanders jr lives on.

2128. Apr. 3, 1780 Thomas Morgan enters 300 ac in Guilford Co on waters of Allemance Cr on middle fork of Rock Cr; "cornering" on David Hopkins E & W line.

2129. Apar. 3, 1780 Mark London enters 250 ac in Guilford Co on Stones fork of Woolf Cr; border: King, conditional line made by John McCabbin & Mark London, head of Fuggals Br, & "near" Taggals (sic) cabbin; includes Chesnut ridge improvement.

page 34
2130. Apr. 3, 1780 William Dent enters 200 ac in Guilford Co on waters of Stinkin Quarter Cr; border: on N by his own survey "that includes" improvement he bought from Non Hamilton.

2131. Apr. 6, 1780 John Purtell (or Pentell) enters 200 ac in Guilford Co on waters of Great Rockhouse Cr; border: his former entrys on NE & N and John Bell on W.

2132. Apr. 8, 1780 Thomas Henderson, John Hamilton, James Hays, & Isaac Wright enter 50 ac in Guilford Co; border: James Martin's deeded land "bought of" John Ragan on S side of Dann R; includes three islands in Dan R.

2133. Apr. 8, 1780 Thomas Henderson, John Hamilton, James Hays, & Isaac Wright enter 10 ac in Guilford Co; includes "the Loan Island" in Dann R; [border:] Valintine Allen on NE and George Oliper (or Olifer) on SW.

2134. Apr. 8, 1780 Francis Worth enters 640 ac in Guilford Co on waters of Brush Cr; includes improvement of Francis Worth on said creek.

2135. Apr. 8, 1780 John Hamilton and Thomas Henderson enters 640 ac in Guilford Co on head waters of Still House Cr; includes some branches of Rockhouse Cr and some of head waters of of Walkers Cr.

2136. Apr. 8, 1780 John Hamilton enters 100 ac in Guilford Co on Horspin Cr; border: former entry made by said Hamilton on said creek on W & N.

2137. Apr. 8, 1780 Minos Cannon enters 220 ac in Guilford Co on waters of Haw R; border: William Buchonon, Mary Asby, John Harry, & James Barns.

2138. Nov. 11, 1780 Richard Lewis enters 200 ac in Guilford Co on waters of Haw R on both sides of Lick Br; border: his own land.

2139. Apr. 13, 1780 Samuel Hatfield enters 160 ac in Guilford Co on Wolf Island Cr; border: Williams, Self, Larkin, Pierpont, & Nobley (or Nolley) Jordan.

2140. Apr. 15, 1780 James Coots enters 200 ac in Guilford Co on Bever Cr; border: Frokock's deeded land.

page 35

2141. Apar. 20, 1780 Andrew Wilson enters 50 ac in Guilford Co; border: on Great road from the Court house to high rock ford and John Chambers SE corner.

2142. Apr. 20, 1780 Michal Witt enters 100 ac in Guilford Co on waters of Redy fork; border: Adam Ramr (sic), Robert Davis, & clament's own line.

2143. Apr. 20, 1780 Adam Ramer enters 50 ac on waters of Redy fork; border: his own land, Mical Witt, & Jacob Swesser (or Sweper).

2144. Apr. 20, 1780 Adam Walker enters 200 ac in Guilford Co; border: a former entry which includes improvement made by Matthew Scott and on both sides of road from Dinis ferry.

2145. Apr. 22, 1780 Robert Peasley enters 200 ac in Guilford Co on waters of Allimance Cr; border: the county line and James Freland.

2146. Apr. 22, 1780 Henry Chambers enters 200 ac in Guilford Co; border: Samuel Denton.

2147. Apr. 22, 1780 John Guner enters 200 ac in Guilford Co between waters of Wolf Island Cr and waters of Dann R; includes his improvement.

2148. Apr. 22, 1780 Henry Chambers enters 150 ac in Guilford Co on waters of Little Town Cr; border: John Swinnon (or Smnnons).

2149. Apr. 22, 1780 Francis Bell enters 200 ac in Guilford Co; border: on S side of "the big road" and N side of Samuel Bell.

2150. Apr. 24, 1780 Robert Means enters 100 ac in Guilford Co; border: on W side of Samuel Dollon.

2151. Apr. 24, 1780 Robert Means enters 100 ac in Guilford Co on waters of Mayo R; border: on E side of Champion Gibson.

2152. Apr. 24, 1780 Isaac Philips enters 150 ac on Great Rockhouse Cr; border: Theophilous Spear on S & E, Brigdale Haney on N, & his former entry.

2153. Apr. 24, 1780 James Sanders enters 100 ac on both sides of Rockhouse Cr; border: his own land on N, Brigdale Haney on E, & Thomas Loyd on W.

page 36

Guilford County, NC, Land Entries 1779-1796

2154. Apr. 24, 1780 John Jones enters 100 ac on N side of Wolf Island Cr; border: Hugh Challus' deeded land on N and Wm Silfon on W.

2155. Apr. 24, 1780 John Pruitt enters 50 ac on N side of Lick fork of Hogans Cr; border: on W of Job Loftis, E side of Samuel Pruit's entry, & runs S.

2156. Apr. 24, 1780 Charles Gilley enters 100 ac on waters of Lick fork of Hogans Cr; border: Hugh Chadlas on S, John Moint on W, & former entry of Edward Elmore on E.

2157. Apr. 24, 1780 Matthew Mills enters 500 ac on W side of Wolf Island Cr; border: Bryant and Mark London's entry; includes Singleton cabbin.

2158. Apr. 24, 1780 Abraham Philips enters 100 ac on waters of big Troublesom Cr; border: James McClellen on N and Robert Small's entry on Glady Br on S; includes head of Camp Br.

2159. May 1, 1780 William James enters 400 ac in Guilford Co on Little Buffelow Br of Matrimony Cr; border: Isaac James.

2160. May 8, 1780 Robert McKimie enters 250 ac in Guilford Co on waters of S Buffellow Cr; border: David Edwards' deeded land and James Wilson's deeded land; includes an improvement.

2161. May 8, 1780 John Brown enters 250 ac in Guilford Co on waters of S Buffellow Cr; border: on both sides of the great road, Ralph Gorrel's NW corner, Thomas Patton, Boyd's entry, & John Duff.

2162. May 9, 1780 Joseph Pain Johnson enters 640 ac in Guilford Co on Little Buffellow Br of Matrimony Cr; border: Henry Grogan.

2163. May 13, 1780 William Dick enters 300 ac in Guilford Co on Gileses Cr waters of Haw R; border: John McKibbin, Wm Matur, John Pritchet, & James Campbell.

page 37
2164. May 15, 1780 Joseph Taylor enters 350 ac in Guilford Co on waters of Sadders Br; border: widow Nelson's entry, his own entry whereon he lives, & entry where John Herbing formerly lived.

2165. May 15, 1780 James Norris enters 60 ac in Guilford Co on waters of Peony Cr; border: Charles Tooney's entry, his own entry, & John Mass' entry.

26

2166. May 16, 1780 Charles Pope enters 200 ac in Guilford Co on head of Deep R; border: Frederick Dun, Isaac Beason, & William Perrison's survey line.

2167. May 16, 1780 Andrew Endsley enters 100 ac in Guilford Co on Bever Cr; border: Thomas Taylor's NW corner, Riaues (or Riaces) line, & Benaman; includes part of an improvement.

2168. May 16, 1780 Samuel Cawhoon enters 200 ac in Guilford Co on Hogans Cr; border: Mical Thomas and Thomas Bowen.

2169. May 16, 1780 John Holladay enters 200 ac in Guilford Co on waters of Troublesom Cr; border: John Flemin and his own land.

2170. May 16, 1780 John Stricklin enters 150 ac in Guilford Co on waters of S Buffellow Cr; border: S line of William Montgomery and Alexander Gray.

2171. May 16, 1780 Jacob Stricklin enters 50 ac in Guilford Co on S Buffellow Cr; border: his own NW corner and David Kern; includes an improvement.

2172. May 16, 1780 Christopher Kobler (or Koleler) enters 200 ac in Guilford Co; border: E corner of his own land and the county line.

2173. May 16, 1780 Robert Morrow enters 200 ac in Guilford Co on waters of Stinkin Quarter Cr; border: on S by county line and on E by Jas Oneal.

2174. May 16, 1780 Joshua Smith enters 100 ac in Guilford Co on both sides of Poppow Cr of Mayo R; border: Samuel Dotton sr on S and Drury Smith on E.

page 38
2175. May 16, 1780 Joshua Smith enters 150 ac in Guilford Co on waters of Mountain Run of Mayo R and Lick fork of Buffalo Island Cr; border: John Gann on E and William Fanning on N.

2176. May 16, 1780 Joshua Smith enters 75 ac in Guilford Co on waters of Tomlins fork and waters of Lick fork both leading into Buffaloe Island Cr; border: John Thomas on S and John Glenn on W.

2177. May 16, 1780 John Gibson enters 100 ac in Guilford Co on White Oak fork waters of Buffaloe Island Cr; border: Winkfield Shopshear on S.

2178. May 16, 1780 John Gibson enters 50 ac in Guilford Co on White Oak fork of Buffalo Island Cr; border: Winkfield Shopshear on N.

2179. May 16, 1780 Isaac Rolston enters 200 ac in Guilford Co on both sides of Dann R; border: Alexander Nelson on W.

2180. May 16, 1780 Joel Mackey enters 300 ac in Guilford Co on waters of Bever Island Cr; border: on NW side of Richard Caldwell.

2181. May 16, 1780 Joel Mackey enters 200 ac in Guilford Co on waters of Shepherds Cr; border: on N side of Elijah Joyce.

2182. May 16, 1780 Samuel Perry enters 300 ac in Guilford Co on Redy fork; border: William Reace and Frohock.

2183. May 16, 1780 Robert Russel enters 25 ac in Guilford Co; border: Thomas Bell on S and his former entry on N.

2184. May 18, 1780 Matthew Mills enters 400 ac in Guilford Co on branches of Wolf Island Cr; border: his own corner, Hugh Challis, & Peter Hutchins' entry.

2185. May 17, 1780 Adam Holker enters 50 ac in Guilford Co on waters of Great Rockhouse Cr; [border:] Alexr Culbreath on E and Samuel Henderson on W.

2186. May 17, 1780 James Hellan enters 50 ac in Guilford Co on waters of Deep R and Abets Cr; border: William Roper's deeded land, Thomas Roper's entry, John Tharpar, & "perhaps" the county line.

page 39
2187. May 17, 1780 Sarah Dawson enters 100 ac in Guilford Co on waters of Redy fork; between entry of Evan Jones on S, entry made by Nathan Dillon on E where Joseph Pirkins lives, entry made by said Evan Jones on N, & Strawhon's line on W.

2188. May 17, 1780 Isaac Heitt enters 640 ac in Guilford Co on waters of Deep R; border: James Caldwell, John Horney, & James Gurdens; includes improvement of John Thomas & Isaac Hiot.

2189. May 17, 1780 David Peeples enters 80 ac in Guilford Co on waters of Jacobs Cr; border: a late survey of said Peeples and entry of Thomas Allen.

2190. May 17, 1780 Robert Crump enters 50 ac in Guilford Co on waters of Long Br of Bever Island Cr; border: the Surry county line.

2191. May 17, 1780 William Washington enters 150 ac in Guilford Co on waters of Hogans Cr; border: Thomas Reden; includes improvement on Poplar Br.

2192. May 18, 1780 Nathaniel Moxley enters 200 ac in Guilford Co on waters of Jacobs Cr; border: corner of former entry of said Moxley.

2193. May 18, 1780 Caleb Hopkins enters 300 ac in Guilford Co on waters of Troublesom Cr; border: on W by Ironworks land, on N by Robert Small & Hugh Lynch, & on E by Doctor Turner.

2194. May 18, 1780 James McKimie enters 400 ac in Guilford Co on both sides of Redy fork of Haw R; includes an improvement.
2195. May 19, 1780 William Smith enters 65 ac in Guilford Co on waters of Allemance Cr; border: his own deeded corner.

2196. May 19, 1780 Francis Maxwell enters 200 ac in Guilford Co on both sides of Blackwood Br.

2197. May 20, 1780 Samuel Averet enters 150 ac in Guilford Co on waters of Buffellow Cr; border: his own old line and John Hoskins deeded line.

page 40
2198. May 20, 1780 Joseph Pain Johnson enters 640 ac in Guilford Co on waters of Matrimony Cr.

2199. May 20, 1780 Joseph Pain Johnson enters 440 ac in Guilford Co on Timber Tree Br; border: on N of Augustus Mills, Henry Grogan, & John Roach.

2200. Jun. 1, 1780 Andrew Law enters 200 ac in Guilford Co on waters of Rocky Br of Rocky Cr; border: his former entry on N and David Hopkins on W.

2201. Jun. 1, 1780 William Montgomery enters 200 ac in Guilford Co; border: his own land on head of Ceader Br.

2202. Jun. 1, 1780 John Healey (or Haley) enters 150 ac in Guilford Co on Patricks Br of Deep R; border: on W side of his former entry.

2203. Jun. 1, 1780 William Trammel enters 200 ac in Guilford Co; border: Jonas Frost, "his" E corner, & William Scott.

2204. Jun. 1, 1780 William Gilmore, for Robert Agnew jr, enters 200 ac in Guilford Co on Rock Cr waters of Allimance Cr; border: claim of Jacob Shearer on S; includes "improvement of an improvement" of Robt Agnew jr aforesaid.

2205. Jun. 2, 1780 Andrew Shirk (or Sherk) enters 150 ac in Guilford Co on N side of Berch Cr of Allimance Cr of Haw R; border: E & W line of Robert Brown's deeded line.

2206. Jun. 17, 1780 John Wilson enters 50 ac in Guilford Co; border: his former (entry--lined out) survey on N and Cornelious Mabery on E.

2207. Jun. 22, 1780 Henry Reed enters 200 ac in Guilford Co on waters of Deep R; border: Stephen Garner's tract on E and William Montgomery's tract on W; includes improvement of Joseph Ballard.

2208. Jun. 22, 1780 Alse Walton enters 600 ac in Guilford Co on waters of Deep R; border: survey of Stephen Gardner on W and survey of Benjamin & Timothy Burnet on N; includes three improvements where old Henry Walton and his two sons lived.

page 41
2209 Jun. 22, 1780 Henry Reed enters 200 ac in Guilford on waters of Deep R; border: deeded land of Stephen (Gardner--lined out) Hayward on W and entry of Resdon Moore on N; includes improvement of John Brazelton.

2210. Jun. 24, 1780 David Gouglas (or Douglas) enters 100 ac in Guilford Co on E side of Mayo R; border: his own land.

2211. Jun. 28, 1780 Joshua Mabey (or Mabery) enters 100 ac in Guilford Co on waters of Mayo R; border: his own land.

2212. Jun. 28, 1780 David Douglas enters 200 (written over 100) ac in Guilford Co; between his own land and James Goings.

2213. Jul. 14, 1780 George Parks enters 300 ac in Guilford Co on waters of Redy fork; border: on N by Simon Moon's improvement and Mr. Strahorn on S; includes improvement of Samuel Britain.

2214. Jul. 20, 1780 John Mars enters 400 ac in Guilford Co on waters of Deep R; border: on N by entry made by Henry Ford.

2215. Aug. 5, 1780 Joshua Smith enters 150 ac in Guilford Co on both sides of Bever (Island--lined out) Cr; border: on E by James Scales, John Whitworth on W, & S by James Scales and Saml Rogers.

2216. Aug. 5, 1780 Samuel Watt enters 100 ac on waters of E side of Hogans Cr; border: claiment's own land and William Oar.

2217. Aug. 5, 1780 David Lovel enters 200 ac in Guilford Co on waters of Little Town Cr and Perry fork; border: John Simmons and Sarah Potter.

2218. Aug. 5, 1780 David Lovel enters 300 ac in Guilford Co on waters of Little Town Cr; "taking in" small improvement of Jn Lovel.

2219. Aug. 5, 1780 David Lovel enters 200 ac in Guilford Co on waters of Fishing Cr; border: his own old entry.

2220. Aug. 5, 1780 David Lovel enters 200 ac in Guilford Co on waters of Town (fork--lined out) Cr and Rockhouse Cr; border: Thomas Noris and John McConney [and or includes] improvement of David Lovel.

page 42
2221. Aug. 9, 1780 Charles Braden enters 13 ac in Guilford Co on waters of N Buffellow Cr; border: W of John Donnill, E of William Hamilton, & S of claiment's land.

2222. Aug. 22, 1780 Samuel Hunter enters 400 ac in Guilford Co on waters of Reed Cr; border: SW corner of John Scales (or Seales).

2223. Aug. 28, 1780 Samuel Parris enters 200 ac in Guilford Co on waters of Great Troublesom Cr on both sides of Camp Br; border: Ironworks tract on S.

2224. Aug. 30, 1780 George Parks enters 300 ac in Guilford Co on waters of Deep R; border: on S by Moses Mendinghall and a former entry of John Sweets; includes improvement of John Campbell.

2225. Sept. 20, 1780 Giles Carter enters 640 ac in Guilford Co on Persimon Br "that falls into" Little Rockhouse Cr and on waters of Great Rockhouse Cr and Little Rockhouse Cr.

2226. Oct. 9, 1780 James Walker enters 500 ac in Guilford Co on waters of Little Allimance Cr; border: Robert Adams and Matthias Amuk; includes widow Walker's improvement.

2227. Oct. 11, 1780 Isham Browder enters 640 ac in Guilford Co on waters of Woolf Island and Toms Creeks; includes John Cooper's improvement.
2228. Nov. 4, 1780 Thomas Person enters 640 ac in Guilford Co on both sides of waters of Hicory Cr; border: his own [land] and others.

2229. Nov. 20, 1780 John Gibson enters 200 ac in Guilford Co; border: Joseph Gibson.

2230. Nov. 21, 1780 Samuel Watt enters 200 ac in Guilford Co on waters of Hogans Cr; between Joseph Pain's entry and Samuel Watt.

2231. Nov. 22, 1780 John Odeneal enters 360 ac in Guilford Co on waters of Wolf Island Cr; border: a former 640 ac entry of claiment's on Quack Quay Br of Wolf Island Cr.

page 43
2232. Nov. 20, 1780 James Barr enters 50 ac in Guilford Co on S side of Redy fork; border: his own land on E, John McClintock, & Edward McGlamey.

2233. Dec. 12, 1780 John Odeneal enters 200 ac in Guilford Co; between James Sanders and Abraham Philips.

2234. Dec. 14, 1780 Barel Brawner enters 250 ac in Guilford Co on waters of Haw R on S side thereof below Wells Ford; border: S end of his own land.

2235. Dec. 25, 1780 Andrew Carmichael enters 100 ac in Guilford Co on waters of Brush (Cr--lined out) fork of Allimance Cr; border: Joseph Dobion and Thomas Alexander.

2236. Jan. 3, 1781 Robert Shaw enters 100 ac in Guilford Co on waters of Allimance Cr; border: entry of Thomas Hamilton jr.

2237. Jan. 6, 1781 Ely Scurry enters 200 ac in Guilford Co on Moses Cr; border: Gideon Johnson.

2238. Jan. 6, 1781 Amos Elord (or Ealord) enters 640 ac in Guilford Co on Quagua Cr; border: begins about 400 yds below his house.

2239. Jan. 6, 1781 James McCullum (or McCuttum) enters 100 ac in Guilford Co on waters of Hogans Cr; border: entry made by Joseph McClean.

2240. Jan. 15, 1781 May Ellitt enters 640 ac in Guilford Co on waters of Little Rockhouse Cr; border: William Ellitt, John McKinny, & Charles Galloway.

2241. Jan. 15, 1781 Stephen Lephew enters 150 ac; border: on N side of his own survey, Benjamin Selmun, & Charles Galloway.

page 44
2242. Jan. 15, 1781 Jacob Boon enters 437 ac in Guilford Co on waters of Cedar Cr "a draught" of Great Allimance Cr; border: runs "according to a former survey and entry is made for in the Earl Granville's office".

2243. Jan. 18, 1781 Joseph Walker enters 100 ac in Guilford Co; border: Edward McGlammary's late survey on N and John Larkin on E.

2244. Jan. 23, 1781 James Fitzgerald enters 150 ac in Guilford Co; border: James Strong, Henry Scales, & Daniel Wilson.

2245. Jun. 23, 1781 Desken Grant enters 300 ac in Guilford Co; border: James Fitzgereld, Thomas Briges, Darby Dallaham, & John Hall.

2246. Jan. 31, 1781 Capt Arthur Forbus enters 500 ac in Guilford Co on waters of Haw R; border: on W and S by his late survey.

"Aug. 19, 1783 entry office opened for Guilford Co."

2247. withdrawn. Aug. 19, 1783 John Balinger enters 60 ac in Guilford Co on waters of Horspin Cr on S side; border: John Hunt "and East" and William Balwin; includes cabbin where Rachel Balinger lives.

2248. Aug. 19, 1783 William Stafford enters 150 ac in Guilford Co on Ryans Cr; border: Thomas Major's survey, Patrick Mullen, James Frazer, & Moses Craner.

2249. Aug. 19, 1783 James McCuistion enters 150 ac in Guilford Co on waters of Hicory Cr; border: William Rogers and Benjamin Bradford.

2250. Aug. 19, 1783 Samuel Frazer enters 250 ac in Guilford Co on S side of Buffalo Cr; border: land formerly belonging to Henry Laferight.

2251. Aug. 20, 1783 William Stafford enters 75 ac in Guilford Co; border: James McGrady on W, Joseph Pirkins, Francis Worth, & William Dillin.

2252. Aug. 20, 1783 Alexander Caldwell enters 197 ac in Guilford Co on dividing ridge between Buffellow and Hicory Creeks; border: Josiah Trotter, William Rogers, Henry Ford, & John Balinger.

page 45
2253. Aug. 20, 1783 Robert Martin enters 150 ac in Guilford Co on waters of SW fork of Jacobs Cr; border: a former entry made on said creek.

2254. Aug. 20, 1780 William Diamond enters 100 ac in Guilford Co on ridge between Bauns Cr and Lick fork Cr; border: Fulkson's corner, Feadyaring, James Hays, David Suttle, Moses Farson, & the Moravins.

2255. Aug. 21, 1780 Elijah Manship enters 200 ac in Guilford Co on Pole cat Cr; border: on W by James Frazer's deeded land, on S by John Hall, & E by John Stewart's claim.

2256. Aug. 21, 1780 Aaron Manship enters 200 ac in Guilford Co on Little Allimance Cr; border: on N by William Barronhill, on E by William Weatherley's deeded land, & on S by John Stewart's claim.

2257. Aug. 25, 1783 Richard Wilson enters 140 ac in Guilford Co on waters of Richland Cr; border: James Denny desc's corner, "his" old field, James McCuistion, Buckhonon, & McElhatten.

2258. Aug. 26, 1783 John Whicker (or Wheeker) enters 90 ac in Guilford Co; border: Thomas Frohock, Charles Bruce, & his own land.

2259. Sept. 1, 1783 John McBride enters 150 ac in Guilford Co on waters of Allimance Cr; border: on E by "said" McDill & John McBride sr, on S by George Coble, & on W by survey of Frederick Craft.

2260. Sept. 3, 1783 Josiah Trotter enters 100 ac in Guilford Co on dividing ridge between John Canaday's deeded land, Robert Green's entry, & widow Williams' claim.

2261. Sept. 6, 1783 James Brown esq enters 500 ac in Guilford Co on S side of big Allimance Cr; border: Tobias Clapp, George Clapp, & Lodwick Clapp.

2262. Sept. 9, 1783 John Forgison enters 166 ac in Guilford Co on Corbeys Cr waters of Dann R; border: Peter Stephens SE corner; includes said Fergison's (sic) improvement.

page 46
2263. Sept. 30, 1783 Jacob Cornet enters 70 ac in Guilford Co on waters of Allimance Cr; border: on N by George Stewart's deeded land, on E by widow Galey, on S by Robert Nealy, & on W by William Quait's deeded land.

2264. Sept. 30, 1783 Abraham McElhatten enters 50 ac in Guilford Co on waters of N Buffellow Cr; border: on N by his own deeded land, on S by Thomas Black, & on W by Ralph Garrel esq; includes spring known as Hindman's Spring.

2265. Oct. 1, 1783 John Isom enters 150 ac in Guilford Co on waters of Allimance Cr; border: on S by Christian Farmer & Andrew Eulmer (or Esalmer), on E by Jacob Star, on N by McCanes, & on W by conditional line.

2266. Oct. 3, 1783 Nathan Thacher enters 200 ac in Guilford Co on waters of Hogans Cr; border: Robert Harris' deeded land and his own survey.

2267. Oct. 10, 1783 Jonathan Bulanger enters 60 ac in Guilford Co on waters of Horspin Cr on S side; border: John Hunt "& East" and William Baldwin; includes cabbin where Rachel Balinger lives.

2268. Oct. 16, 1783 Mary Porter enters 300 ac in Guilford Co on waters of Great Troublesom Cr; border: Col. Little's former entry now in possession of Francis McBride "at NE corner".

2269. Oct. 16, 1783 Francis McBride enters 96 ac in Guilford Co on big Troublesom Cr; border: said McBride, James Flack, & James Lanear.

2270. Oct. 16, 1780 William Gamble enters 40 ac on E side of Allimance Cr; between John Philip Clapp, Glass Clapp on N, & Glass' on S.

2271. Oct. 16, 1783 Michael Mason enters 242 ac in Guilford Co on Reddocks Cr and S Buffeloe Cr; border: E & W line of John Ballinger and Richard Williams.

2272. Oct. 17, 1783 Rev David Caldwell enters 328 ac in Guilford Co on waters of Mordicais Cr; border: SW corner of land of William Greer desc.

page 47
2273. Oct. 17, 1783 Charles Bruce esq enters 100 ac in Guilford Co on waters of Troublesom Cr; border: his own land and Minos Cannon.

2274. Oct. 17, 1783 Charles Bruce esq enters 250 ac in Guilford Co on both sides of Falls Cr; includes a mill seat; border: Surry county line on W.

2275. Oct. 23, 1783 Alexander Caldwell enters 317 ac in Guilford Co; between Robert Green, John Canady, widow Williams, James Wilson, David Edwards, & Michael Mason.

2276. caveated by said(?) Cantril; caveat ruled good; withdrawn. Oct. 25, 1783 Leven Mitchel enters 150 ac in Guilford Co on waters of Woolf Island Cr on S side; border: John Grunger.
2277. Oct. 25, 1783 Leven Mitchel enters 200 ac in Guilford Co on waters of Woolf Island Cr on S side; border: widow Browder.

2278. Oct. 31, 1783 Henry Cobb enters 200 ac in Guilford Co; border: his own land and Nicholas Gift.

2279. Nov. 1, 1783 Minos Cannon enters 197 ac in Guilford Co on both sides of his own spring branch; border: his own [land] and Benjamin Stone.

2280. withdrawn. Nov. 1, 1783 Levin Mitchel enters 100 ac in Guilford Co on Silver fork which enpties into Town Cr; border: Charles Toney & runs up the creek.

2281. withdrawn. Nov. 1, 1783 Levin Mitchel enters 46 ac in Guilford Co on W branch of Silver fork "that enters into" Town Cr and runs up the branch.

2282. Nov. 4, 1783 Jacob Cantrel enters 170 ac in Guilford Co on N fork of Wolf Island Cr; border: John Granger on N side; includes two small improvements.

2283. Nov. 4, 1783 Lawrence Bankston enters 300 ac in Guilford Co on waters of Wolf Island Cr; border: Nathaniel Newman, Isaac Cantrell, & Lander's "agreement line".

page 48
2284. Nov. 4, 1783 Lawrence Bankson enters 150 ac in Guilford Co on Wolf Island Cr; border: his "open" line.

2285. Nov. 4, 1783 John Linder enters 100 ac in Guilford Co on waters of Wolf Island Cr; border: his own corner.

2286. Nov. 4, 1783 John Cantrell enters 400 ac in Guilford Co on Wolf Island Cr; border: Isham Browder and James Wardlaw's "agreement" line.

2287. Nov. 4, 1783 Sarah Marsh enters 300 ac in Guilford Co on waters of Hickory Cr and Poll catt Cr; border: John McAdow's N & S line and Cain Cr road; includes improvement said Sarah Marsh lives on.

2288. Nov. 5, 1783 James Lord enters 100 ac in Guilford Co on both sides of Wolf Island Cr; border: on W by William Young, on S by John McCarrell jr, & on W by William Harrison.

2289. Nov. 5, 1783 Bethuel Coffin enters 130 ac in Guilford Co on waters of Horspin Cr; border: Robert Galbraith on S side, David Massey on N, & his own land on E.

2290. caveated by Robert Ferguson; caveat withdrawn. Nov. 10, 1783 John Ferguson enters 100 ac in Guilford Co on waters of Town Cr; border: Charles Toney's old line and runs up the creek.

2291. Nov. 10, 1783 Leven Mitchel enters 75 ac in Guilford Co on W branch of Town Cr which branch is called Piney Br; includes "a notable spring" at head of branch.

2292. Nov. 12, 1783 William Miller enters 100 ac in Guilford Co on head of Piney Cr; border: on S of his own deeded land and E of Isaac Wright.

2293. Nov. 17, 1783 Jesse Williams enters 640 ac in Guilford Co on waters of S Buffaloe Cr; border: SW corner of David Edwards' deeded land, Asa Hunt's deeded land, & "line made by entry of James Archer on land where George Hiett lives".

2294. Nov. 17, 1783 John Walker enters 300 ac in Guilford Co on waters of Great Rockhouse Cr; border: Thomas Carter, Jesse Morton, Benjamin Selman, James Roberts, & said John Walker.

page 49
2295. Nov. 18, 1783 Tilman Creadelbough enters 250 ac in Guilford Co on branch of Rich fork of Abets Cr; border: county line and William Davis; includes his improvement.

2296. Nov. 18, 1783 Jesse Williams enters 200 ac in Guilford Co on dividing ridge between Horspin & S Buffaloe Creeks; includes some springs of S Buffaloe Cr; border: Timothy Russell's deeded land, Richard Williams' deeded land, entry of James Archer, & land where George Hiatt lives.

2297. Nov. 18, 1783 James Butle enters 146 ac in Guilford Co; border: William Rogers' corner, Hickory Cr, & Brown.

2298. Nov. 18, 1783 William Roberson enters 60 ac in Guilford Co on head of County line Cr; border: Hugh Gwin, William Hall, John Tailor, & Joseph Pane.

2299. withdrawn. Nov. 18, 1783 Hance Hamilton enters 200 ac in Guilford Co on waters of Reedy fork; border: deeded land of Cunningland (sic), Thompson, & a former entry of Thos Linsey desc.

2300. withdrawn. Nov. 18, 1783 Hance Hamilton enters 200 ac in Guilford Co on waters of Moons Cr of Brushy fork; border: deeded land on Richard Moon, "his" lines of entry formerly made by Major John Nelson, & entry formerly made by Thos Linsy desc.

2301. "with". Nov. 19, 1783 James Billingsly enters 277 ac in Guilford Co on waters of Marris (or Harris) fork; border: deed from state to Thomas Lincey desc; includes improvement where John Hinslett (? write over) formerly lived.

2302. withdrawn. Nov. 19, 1783 Hance Hamilton enters 640 (write over) ac in Guilford Co on waters of Meares fork; border: deed from state to Thomas Lincey desc; includes improvement where James Oliphant formerly lived.

2303. Nov. 19, 1783 Hance Hamilton enters 70 ac in Guilford Co on waters of Richland Cr; border: deed by James McCuiston to Thomas Linsey; includes improvement where Hance Hamilton lives.

2304. withdrawn £5 paid, £15 J Johnson, £20 paid. Nov. 19, 1783 Joel Sanders enters 400 ac in Guilford Co on waters of Deep R; border: deeded land of John Sanders sr, Edward Bond, & entry made by William Dent jr.

2305. Nov. 19, 1783 Joseph Lovel enters 200 ac in Guilford Co on waters of Pole cat Cr; border: William Williams' deeded line, Henry Porter, William Bumhen, & William Kelly.

page 50
2306. Nov. 20, 1783 Isaac Lenager enters 270 ac in Guilford Co on waters of Abbets Cr; border or near: the Rowan [County] line and joins James Henderson and widow Gilleand (or Gilbrand).

2307. £14.6 paid back A Cook for 147 ac def(?). Nov. 21, 1783 Abraham Cook enters 300 ac in Guilford Co on waters of Deep R; border: on E side of entry of Smith Moore, on S side Isaac Beeson's deeded land, John Hamilton, & Thomas Henderson.

2308. Nov. 28, 1783 Constant Perkins enters 300 ac in Guilford Co; border: on N side of Ironworks land.

2309. Dec. 4, 1783 Leven Russel enters 405 ac in Guilford Co on waters of Little Rockhouse Cr; border: Kimbral; includes John Kembral's improvement.

2310. withdrawn. Dec. 4, 1783 Richard Covington enters 200 ac in Guilford Co on waters of Little Rockhouse Cr; border: George Kimbral, Rev. David Caldwell, Jacob Barnet, & Robert Call.

2311. Dec. 8, 1783 Eleazer Kersey enters 450 ac in Guilford Co on both sides of Richland Cr; border: Arthur Carey; includes improvement where said Kersey lives.

2312. Dec. 13, 1783 Obadiah Harris enters 250 ac in Guilford Co on waters of Deep R on Bobbs Br; between John Stewart and John Balwin; includes Silas Murphey's improvement.

2313. withdrawn. Dec. 15, 1783 Moses Craner enters 100 ac in Guilford Co on waters of Hickory Cr; border: on W side of Robert Erwin where "he" lives.

2314. Dec. 20, 1783 William Way enters 130 ac in Guilford Co on waters of Hickory Cr; border: William Brown, William Rogers, Henry Ford, & "his" own late entry.

2315. Dec. 20, 1783 James Anthony enters 150 ac in Guilford Co on waters of Hickory Cr; border: (William B_?_ --lined out) John Osborn; includes old improvement of said Anthony.

2316. Dec. 20, 1783 William Shaw and Robert Shaw enters 200 ac in Guilford Co; border: Matthias Anrack's S or E line.

page 51
2317. Dec. 20, 1783 Andrew Conner enters 400 ac in Guilford Co on head of Cabbin Br "a draught" of Reedy fork; border: Moses Strahan and up both sides of branch; includes his own improvement.

2318. Dec. 23, 1783 Joseph Land enters 105 ac in Guilford Co on both sides of Long Br waters of Great Rockhouse Cr.

2319. Dec. 23, 1783 Abraham Philips enters 150 ac in Guilford Co on waters of Great Troublesom Cr; border: James Lay on S and John Harne (or Hamer).

2320. Dec. 23, 1783 Jacob Philips enters 150 ac in Guilford Co on waters of Troublesom Cr; border: Alexr Brown and James & Thos Massey.

2321. Dec. 27, 1783 Hugh Shannon enters 40 ac in Guilford Co on waters of Hogens Cr; border: his own line, Charles Dean, John Smith (or Suth), & county line.

2322. Dec. 27, 1783 William Liester enters 40 ac in Guilford Co; border: Saml Nelson, Isaac Weatherley, Thomas Lander, & John Elliot.

2323. Jan. 9, 1784 William Leslie enters 100 ac in Guilford Co on waters of Great Allamance Cr; border: on N by Robert Morrow, on E by William Dent, & on Jeremiah Fields; includes a small improvement.

2324. withdrawn 30£ paid 8£6 (blank) £38.7 total(sic). Jan. 10, 1784 John Job & John Mairs enters 400 ac in Guilford Co on waters of Allamance Cr; border: on N by Job and on S by Tobias Clap.

2325. Jan. 26, 1784 William Gamble enters 100 ac in Guilford Co on waters of Allamance Cr; border: Robert Morrow, William Dent, & Thadues Bell.

2326. withdrawn. Jan. 29, 1784 Joseph Payn enters 200 ac in Guilford Co on waters of & N side of Hogans Cr; border: his own E corner and John Hodges.

2327. Jan. 27, 1784 Joseph Payn enters 200 ac in Guilford Co; border: on his own S line near mouth of James Walker's Br and a conditional line.

page 52
2328. Feb. 3, 2784 Elijah Charles enters 150 ac in Guilford Co; border: on vacant land on S and on E side of land he lives on.

2329. Feb. 3, 1784 William Dillon enters 20 ac in Guilford Co on waters of Richland Cr; border: his late entry, Arthur Forbes, & Jams McCuiston.

2330. Feb. 16, 1784 William Walker enters 40 ac in Guilford Co on branch of & S side of Dan R; between Peter Fore and William Cromp.

2331. withdrawn; being no(?) land to pay in case the Treasurer allows it. Feb. 17, 1784 John Walker enters 100 ac in Guilford Co on waters of Reedy fork; border: John Peorry's E corner, Caleb Isop, & his line.

2332. executed(?) & sold by Vandal & purchased by George Coble of James Dill issued(?) in Geo Coble's name. Feb. 17, 1784 John Smith enters 40 ac in Guilford Co on waters of Allamance Cr; border: on NW side of George Coble which "he" bought from John Phips between said land and Finley Shaw's survey.

2333. [not in book; skip in the numbers.]

2334. Feb. 18, 1784 Nathaniel Lanier enters 100 ac in Guilford Co on waters of Great Troublesom Cr; border: Francis McBride, John Franlkner, & James Lanier desc.

2335. Feb. 18, 1784 Robert Walker enters 260 ac in Guilford Co on waters of Big Rockhouse Cr; border: near James Sanders.

2336. Feb. 18, 1784 William Wiley enters 100 ac in Guilford Co; border: Hugh Wiley's corner, his own line, & John Toms.

2337. Mar. 4, 1784 Jesse Parker enters 125 ac in Guilford Co on waters of Reedy fork of Haw R known as Maxwells Br; border: Nathaniel Simpson on S.

2338. Mar. 5, 1784 Isaac Beeson enters 180 ac in Guilford Co on waters of Deep R; border: Joseph Miller, Abraham Cook, & land where said Beeson lives.

2339. Mar. 6, 1784 Thomas Moore enters 150 ac in Guilford Co; border: on S side of tract of John Healey where Isaac Widows lives, on W of Jeremiah Shelley "that was taken by" Bemett (sic) Bradford, & on N of John Healey's "home" deeded land.

page 53
2340. Mar. 6, 1784 John Healey enters 150 ac in Guilford Co; border: on S side of Jeremiah Shelley's "taken by" Bennet Bradford and on E of where "I" live.
2341. Mar. 10, 1784 Isaac Linegar enters 100 ac in Guilford Co on Willsons Cr; border or near: the Rowan [County] line.

2342. Mar. 10, 1784 Andrew Law enters 19 ac in Guilford Co on Rock Cr; border: Mayon, Francis Maxwell and John Montgomery.

2343. Mar. 11, 1784 Isaac Newman enters 91 ac in Guilford Co on waters of Hickory Cr; border: John Ozburn.

2344. Mar. 11, 1784 Hezekiah Sanders enters 50 ac in Guilford Co on waters of Deep R; border: deeded land of Thomas Mills and Amos Mills; includes improvement made by Ely Thornton.

2345. Mar. 29, 1784 Massey Maderis enters 50 ac in Guilford Co on "drains" of Beleus Cr waters; border: on ridge between George Cumming, John Lowry, & claimant's land.

2346. Apr. 8, 1784 Samuel Thompson enters 20 ac in Guilford Co on Reedy fork of Haw R; border: John Cunningham and Robert Thompson; includes an island between said tracts.

2347. Apr. 10, 1784 Zaza (sic) Brasher enters 100 ac in Guilford Co on waters of Jacobs Cr; includes William Kirkpatrick's old smith shop "improvement"; border: Moksby and Mullins improvement.

2348. Apr. 10, 1784 Asa Brasher enters 100 ac in Guilford Co on waters of Jacobs Cr; border: a mill seat, "my" own land, & Saml Short.

2349. Apr. 10, 1784 Asa Brasher enters 100 ac in Guilford Co on waters of Jacobs Cr; border: Zaza Brasher and James Hays.

2350. Apr. 10, 1784 Thomas Archer enters 100 ac in Guilford Co on waters of Deep R; border: William Morland on S, James Hays on E, & his own land on N; includes an island between said tracts.

2351. Apr. 12, 1784 Luke Barnett enters 70 ac in Guilford Co on W side of Great Rockhouse Cr; border: Daniel Wall on W and land where said Barnett lives.

page 54
2352. Apr. 18, 1784 John Cumming enters 85 ac in Guilford Co on S side of Big Troublesom Cr; border: his own corner and Thos Lomax.

2353. Apr. 27, 1784 William Plunkett enters 40 ac in Guilford Co on waters of Stinking Quarter Cr; border: his own land, Andrew Shatterlin, & Peter Ingolls.

2354. Apr. 27, 1784 William Adam Short enters 130 ac in Guilford Co on waters of Big Troublesom Cr; border and between: Thomas Massey & widow Short "now" Sarah Green.

2355. Apr. 29, 1784 William Kelly enters 150 ac in Guilford Co on waters of Pole cat Cr; border: on W by Joh (sic) Hall's deeded land, on N by Aaron Manship's survey, & on E by John Stewart's claim.

2356. withdrawn. May 19, 1784 Sherwood Foney enters 200 ac in Guilford Co on waters of Dan R; includes said Foney's improvement where he lives.

2357. May 21, 1784 Jeremiah Fields enters 300 ac in Guilford Co on waters of Allamance Cr; border: on S & W of land where said Fields lives.
2358. May 26, 1784 William Horney enters 16 ac in Guilford Co on waters of Deep R; border: land where Mary Mendingall lives and land of Samuel Hartgrave.

2359. Jun. 22, 1784 George Stewart enters 50 ac in Guilford Co on waters of Land Cr of Reedy fork; border: Samuel Drick, Joseph McDowel, & James White.

2360. Jun. 23, 1784 James Johnson enters 50 ac in Guilford Co on waters of Deep R; border: on E corner of land formerly property of Hier Mills.

2361. Jul. 19, 1784 Edward Tatum (or Tatom) enters 65 ac in Guilford Co on ridge between waters of Haw R and Mears fork of both sides of Bruce's road; border: Peter Harris, Joseph Hoskins, Nathal Peeples, & place where John Tatum resides.

2362. Jul. 20, 1784 Joseph Potter enters 100 ac in Guilford Co on waters of Town Cr on Piney fork; border: David Lovel and Joel Gunter; includes "plantation" where he lives.

page 55
2363. withdrawn; money returned. Jul. 26, 1784 Bethewel Coffin enters 96 ac in Guilford Co on waters of Horsepin Cr; border: Arnold Hoskins on E, Robert Galbreath on W, & John Kembley on N.

2364. withdrawn fee due(?). Jul. 28, 1784 John Farrington enters 100 ac in Guilford Co on waters of Brush Cr "a draught" of Reedy fork; border: Thomas Thornbrough, Allen Anthank, & James McGuady.

2365. Jul. 30, 1784 Robert Galbraith and Arnold Hoskins enter 100 ac in Guilford Co on waters of Horsepin Cr; border: E & N side of said Galbraith's deeded land, on E of said Hoskins, & on S of John Kembley's land.

2366. Aug. 13, 1784 Joseph Hyatt enters 200 ac in Guilford Co on waters of Deep R on W side; border: NE corner of George Parks survey and widow Carsey.

2367. Aug. 13, 1784 George Jameson enters 100 ac in Guilford Co; border: on N of Parks, Joseph Hyatt, & branch known as Hay Br.

2368. withdrawn; money returned. Aug. 16, 1784 William Stafford enters 45 ac in Guilford Co on waters of Brush Cr; border: his own late entry.

2369. Aug. 16, 1784 William Gowdy esq enters 70 ac in Guilford Co on waters of Reedy fork; border: on W side of his own survey.

2370. withdrawn; money returned. Aug. 16, 1784 Benjamin Shaw enters 47 ac in Guilford Co on waters of Reedy fork; border: his own land on S side, W side of survey Willm Shefferd bought of Thos Henderson, on N of Jonathan Knight, & on E of Stangeman Stanley.

2371. Aug. 13, 1784 Frederick Cobler enters 50 ac in Guilford Co on Matrimony Cr on N side of Dan R; border: Ctrustdc(?) Cobler and Henry Grogan.

2372. Aug. 17, 1784 David Crew enters 150 ac in Guilford Co on head waters of Deep R; border: Charles Pape, Isaac Beeson, & Surry County line; includes his improvement.

2373. Aug. 17, 1784 Mary Brasilton, for her son John Brasilton, enters 100 ac in Guilford Co; border: on S side of Henry Reed's late survey and on E side of John Healey.
page 56
2374. Aug. 20, 1784 Owen Herrin enters 45 ac in Guilford Co on both sides of Long Br of Great Rockhouse Cr; border: Alexr Colbreath, James Richey, & Richd Mason.

2375. Aug. 21, 1784 William Thomas enters 165 ac in Guilford Co on waters of Lick fork of Buffaloe Island Cr; border: Willm Thomas on S, Jonathan Norton on W, & Joseph Gibson on N.

2376. Aug. 25, 1784 Benjamin Brittain enters 300 ac in Guilford Co on waters of Reedy fork of Haw R; border: Willm Robinson on E, Drury Peeples on N, James Leaper on W, & Abner Hunt on N; includes his own improvement.

2377. "by order of court". Aug. 25, 1784 Thomas Gossett enters 400 ac in Guilford Co on Little Hickory Cr waters of Deep R; border: Osbrom, Brown, Ozbum, & Reynolds.

2378. Aug. 25, 1784 Daniel Ozborn enters 380 ac in Guilford Co on Little Hickory Cr waters of Deep R; border: Willm Reynolds, Gansel, Pearson, & others.

2379. Aug. 30, 1784 William Beals enters 150 ac in Guilford Co on waters of Pole Cat Cr; border: John Beal jr, Peter Dicker (or Dickies), & John Stone; includes improvement where John Bond use to live.

2380. Sept. 7, 1784 William Shannon enters 100 ac in Guilford Co; border: William Dickey's N corner and Bare Barker.

2381. Sept. 27, 1784 John Talbot enters 400 ac in Guilford Co on both sides of N fork of Deep R; border: on S side of road from New Garden to George Mendingall's mill "agreeable to" division line concluded on James Mendingall and the claimant; includes his own improvement.

2382. Sept. 28, 1784 John Stewart enters 400 ac in Guilford Co on waters of Allamance and Pole cat Creeks; border: on N by William Neatherly, on W by Fodegell's old line, on S by William Shannon, & on E by John Wiley and William Quiet.

page 57
2383. Sept. 30, 1784 Minos Cannon enters 150 ac in Guilford Co on waters of Jacobs Cr; border: Peter Mitchell's W line and on Thos Nil's S line.

2384. Sept. 30, 1784 Robert Lamb enters 150 ac in Guilford Co on waters of Pole cat Cr; border: land where he lives and Wilson.

2385. Oct. 4, 1784 Ephraim Thomson enters 100 ac in Guilford Co on waters of Jacobs Cr; border: Lewis Peeples' W line.

2386. Oct. 22, 1784 John Gildcrests (or Gilcrest) enters 100 ac in Guilford Co on waters of Reedy fork on S side said creek; border: on E by land where claimant lives and on W by John McClintick.

2387. Oct. 24, 1784 Joseph Allen enters 100 ac in Guilford Co; border: Alexander Walker, Joseph Pain, & Joshua Wright.

2388. Oct. 25, 1784 John Clark enters 58 ac in Guilford Co on both sides of Brush Cr; includes vacant land between Daniel Brittain, Aaron Mendingall, William White jr, & the said Jno Clark's deeded land.

2389. Oct. 25, 1784 Jacob Hunt enters 400 ac in Guilford Co on waters of Moores Cr and Brush Cr; border: George Rail, Joshua Edwards, John Clark, Wm White jr, & Richd Moon.

2390. Oct. 25, 1784 Asa Brasher enters 40 ac in Guilford Co on ridge between Haw R and Troublesom Cr; border: S of Moses Campbell's deeded land and N of Fredk Dill's deeded land.

2391. Oct. 27, 1784 Nathaniel Linder enters 150 ac in Guilford Co on N fork of Bald (or Bold) Run waters of Rockhouse Cr; border: James Landers and John Pirkle.

2392. Nov. 16, 1784 Andrew Hall enters 208 ac in Guilford Co on waters of Rosses Cr; border: John Starratt, Rachel Wilson, James Wright, & former survey of said Hall; includes part of improvement where he lives.

2393. Nov. 16, 1784 Nathan Dillin enters 100 ac in Guilford Co on head waters (write over) of Haw R; border: John Endsley jr's (write over) former entry on N, Nathan Moor's entry on E, & James Ollifant's entry on W.

page 58
2394. Nov. 17, 1784 John Wafford enters 80 ac in Guilford Co on Troublesom Cr; border: Thomas Holgan, James Johnson, William Wallace, Michael Caffey, Reorge (sic) Roland, & John Conn.

2395. Nov. 25, 1784 Thomas Henderson enters 80 ac in Guilford on waters of Walkers Cr; border: entry of Alexander McClarans on E & S.

2396. Nov. 20, 1784 (sic) James Hunter enters 150 ac in Guilford Co on branches on N side of Bever Island Cr; border: his own [land] and John Joyce.

2397. Jan. 11, 1785 James Thompson enters 200 ac in Guilford Co on waters of Deep R; border: John Hamilton's E & W line.

2398. Jan. 11, 1785 Gager Starbuck enters 25 ac in Guilford Co on waters of Redy fork; border: on E by land where he lives and on W by land where Samuel Frasher lives.

2399. Jan. 12, 1785 Matthew Coffin enters 20 ac in Guilford Co on both sides of Redy fork; border: Gager Starbuck on E, Matthew Coffin on W, Charles Bruce on N, & Edward Bullock on S.

2400. Jan. 12, 1785 Nathan Marony enters 100 ac in Guilford Co; border: John Ros "his" E & W line and Foton.

2401. Jan. 15, 1785 Moses Barrow enters 250 ac in Guilford Co on both sides of Kerbies Cr waters of Deep R; border: John Forgeson's entry.

2402. Jan. 17, 1784 Caleb Jessop enters 40 ac in Guilford Co on waters of Redy fork; border: his own [land], John Sanders "or" Matthew Coffin's W line, Ebenesor & John Perry's E line, & John Wrecker's E line.

2403. Jan. 19, 1785 William Montgomery enters 300 ac in Guilford Co on waters of Buffolo and Rock Creeks; border: entry of claimant, John Gilbert, Nicholas Gift, & John Montgomery.

2404. Jan. 26, 1785 Daniel Crues (or Cruie) enters 100 ac in Guilford Co on head waters of Deep R; border: on N side of former entry of said Crues.

2405. 44 ac deficient; to return £2 in case the Treasurer allows it. Jan. 27, 1785 Moses Craner enters 183 ac in Guilford Co on S Buffellow and Pole cat Creeks; border: on E corner of William Williams survey, James Frazer, Henry Porter, & Moses Craner.

page 59
2406. Jan. 27, 1785 John McAdow enters 100 ac in Guilford Co on waters of N Buffalo Cr; border: W corner on William Hall's survey.

2407. withdrawn being no land warrant to be returned & money paid back. Feb. 8, 1785 Thomas Stewart enters 50 ac in Guilford Co on waters of Richland Cr; border: on E end of entry made by Samuel Duck, on S by land where Robert Craig lives, & land where Jas McCuistion lives.

2408. Feb. 9, 1785 Josiah Trotter enters 100 ac in Guilford Co on waters of Hicory Cr; border: land where claimant lives and late survey of heirs of Alexr Caldwell.

2409. Feb. 12, 1785 Thomas Stewart enters 70 ac in Guilford Co on waters of Richland Cr; border: a late survey of Samuel Duck and tract belonging to heirs of William Denney.

2410. Feb. 14, 1785 Joshua Wright enters 100 ac on waters of Hogans Cr; border: on S of John Hodgins' E & W line and land where claimant lives.

2411. Feb. 16, 1785 John Lewis enters 150 ac in Guilford Co on ridge between Hogans Cr and Little Troublesom Cr; border: on E side of James Nichols, William Denney, & Joseph Chapman.

2412. Feb. 17, 1785 Edward Millis enters 73 ac in Guilford Co on waters of Buffelow and Pole cat Creeks; border: Thomas Mager, James Frazer, & Patrick Mullen.

2413. Feb. 18, 1785 Jonathan Howel enters 100 ac in Guilford Co on Watters Run on E side; border: Patrick Horney.

2414. Feb. 22, 1785 George Neas (or Nees) enters 50 ac in Guilford Co on waters of Allamance Cr; border: on E by his own land, On S by Jacob Strickland, & N by William Albright.

2415. Feb. 22, 1785 John Walker enters 100 ac in Guilford Co on N side of Dann R; border: William Walker and Nathaniel Hoggatt; known as Niles Bent.

2416. Feb. 22, 1785 Benjamin Going enters 100 ac in Guilford Co on waters of Popaw Cr of Mayo R; border: Bartholomew Grogan and Oniel Fields.

2417. Feb. 22, 1785 Joseph Pain enters 200 ac in Guilford Co; border: John Allen's S corner, a branch of Troublesom Cr, his own line, Isaac Low, & James Nichols.

pag 60
2418. Feb. 22, 1785 Thomas Allen enters 180 ac in Guilford Co on waters of Prewet's fork of Hogans Cr.

2419. Feb. 23, 1785 John Ozia enters 200 ac in Guilford Co on waters of Reedy fork; border: on W by Henry Hart, on S by John Trolinger, on E by John Harper; includes improvement of George Lawrance.

2420. Feb. 23, 1785 Samuel Knight enters 40 ac in Guilford Co on head waters of Deep R; border: Abel Knight's deeded land on N, Benj Hartgroves on W, & Martin Pegg on S.

2421. Feb. 23, 1785 John Ozia enters 50 ac in Guilford Co on waters of Redy fork; border: on W by widow Nelson and on S by Daniel Hopkins.

2422. Feb. 23, 1785 John Hawkins enters 200 ac in Guilford Co on Quaker fork of Allemance Cr; border: on S side of his own deeded land; includes his claim.

2423. Feb. 23, 1785 Edward Richardson enters 20 ac in Guilford Co; border: Walter Hill, William Robinson, & James Craiton.

2424. Feb. 25, 1785 Alexander Martin enters 100 ac in Guilford Co on Brushey fork of Jacobs Cr; between Isaac Perryman and land said Alexr Martin bought of Robert Rolston.

2425. Feb. 25, 1785 William Gray enters 150 ac in Guilford Co on waters of Redy fork of Deep R; border: his own line, Isaac Beeson, Abraham Cook, John Hamilton, & Thos Henderson (following is lined out: Daniel Fulton, James Flack, John Rosen, & William Meroney).

2426. Feb. 26, 1785 Nathan Maroney enters 200 ac in Guilford Co on waters of Redy fork of Haw R; border: Samuel Fulton, James Flack, John Rosen, & William Meroney.

2427. Feb. 28, 1785 William Hiett enters 80 ac on waters of Horspin Cr; border: S end of his land and Assa Hunt.

page 61
2428. Mar. 1, 1785 John Cox enters 30 ac in Guilford Co on waters of Allemance Cr; border: William Quait, John Steward, Robert Nealey, Jacob Kennett.

2429. Mar. 2, 1785 Timothey Macy enters 360 ac in Guilford Co on Bull Run branch of Deep R; border: on S by John Macy, on W by Reuben Bunker, on N by Samuel Frazer.

2430. Mar. 5, 1785 Smith Moore enters 300 ac in Guilford Co; between Phbe Mendingall's deeded land and Randolph County line; includes improvement where James Medcalf did live.

2431. Mar. 5, 1785 Thomas Benbow enters 100 ac in Guilford Co on waters of Deep R; border: N & S line of his own land.

2432. Mar. 7, 1785 William Brown enters 150 ac in Guilford Co on N fork of Deep R; border: his own land, Benjamin Harigroves, Abel Knight, William Stafford, & Jonathan Knight.

2433. Mar. 9, 1785 Jonas Reehs enters 200 ac in Guilford Co on waters of Deep R on S side; border: William Brazelton's old deeded land.

2434. Mar. 9, 1785 Peter Helton enters 150 ac in Guilford Co on Ruddocks Cr; border: James Helton's late survey and Joseph Gun.

2435. Mar. 12, 1785 Jerimiah Fields enters 300 ac in Guilford Co; border: on N side of John Hawkins old line and tract that formerly belonged to Joseph Fields.

2436. Mar. 12, 1785 Samuel Fields enters 400 ac in Guilford Co on waters of Allimance, Pole cat, & Sandey Creeks; border: at SW corner of old tract "called" Robert Fields and John Fields.

page 62
2437. Mar. 19, 1785 Allen Williams enters 150 ac in Guilford Co on waters of Wolf Island Cr; border: on E by said Williams and on S by Sutton McCollister.

2438. Mar. 21, 1785 Richard Wilson enters 40 ac in Guilford Co; border: on W of Robert Craig and his own place.

2439. Mar. 23, 1785 Jonathan Gifford enters 400 ac in Guilford Co on waters of Deep R; border: George Hiet and on S side of Risdon Moore; includes "George Beard's improvement Richard Beard's" and improvement where claimant lives.

2440. Mar. 25, 1785 Eleazer Hunt enters 100 ac in Guilford Co on waters of Horspin Cr; border: land where Eleazer Hunt lives, the late Thomas Jessop, Timothey Russel, & Asa Hunt.

2441. Mar. 28, 1785 William Gray enters 50 ac in Guilford Co on waters of Muddy fork of Deep R; border: Williamson Brown, Benjm Hairgrove, Abel Knight, & Martin Pegg.

2442. Mar. 28, 1785 John Walton enters 200 ac in Guilford Co on S side of Deep R; border: conditional line between widow Walton & Evan Harris, John Brown, & the county line.

2443. Mar. 29, 1785 William Reynolds enters 640 ac in Guilford Co on Little Hicory Cr and Russels Run; border: N line of deeded land where he lives; includes improvement where William Leonard did live.

page 63
2444. Mar. 29, 1785 Isaac Widdows enters 300 ac in Guilford Co on waters of Richland Cr or Mordicais Cr; border: Philip Reddings and widow Pidgeon.

2445. Mar. 29, 1785 Jonas Ricks enters 100 ac in Guilford Co on waters of Mordicais Cr; border: Joseph Hoggatt and John Huley.

2446. Mar. 31, 1785 Edward Brewer enters 100 ac in Guilford Co; being surplus land of tract bought from George Jude; border: Batts Lacy.

2447. Apr. 4, 1785 Leven Gray enters 400 ac in Guilford Co on N side of Ridge fork; border: W of Robert Russel jr and E of Samuel Maxwell.

2448. Apr. 5, 1785 Jacob Troak enters 294 ac in Guilford Co on head of Travis Cr of Haw R; border: on N by Jacob Sumers, on W by Shaimuher & Summers, & on S by Troay's (sic) own land.

2449. withdrawn money returned. Apr. 8, 1785 Josiah Tomlinson enters 360 ac in Guilford Co on waters of Rich fork of Abbots Cr; border: Rowan county line; includes improvements where said Tomlinson lives.

2450. Apr.13, 1785 Matthew Coffin enters 80 ac in Guilford Co on waters of Richland Cr waters of Deep R; border: his own [land] on W, Elijah Charles on N, Joseph Hoggatt on E, & James Mendinghall on S.

2451. Apr. 19, 1785 William Denny enters 56 ac in Guilford Co on waters of Allmance Cr; border: on S by his own line, on W by John McClane, on N by Jesse McComb, & on E by Henry Barnhart.

2452. Apr. 21, 1785 Evan Harris enters 150 ac in Guilford Co on Deep R; border: NW corner of George Person's deeded land, William Montgomery, & crossing Deep R.

page 64
2453.Apr. 26, 1785 Henry Pitt enters 100 ac in Guilford Co on waters of Rich fork; border: John Veach's corner, Josiah Tomlinson, & the county line.

2454. Apr. 28, 1785 Hance Clerk enters 100 ac in Guilford Co on waters of Allimance Cr; border: on N by deeded land of Matthew Eniuk.

2455. Apr. 30, 1785 Philip Coble enters 117 ac in Guilford Co; border: on E by George Summerman, on N by Bostion Garringer, & on W by entry of Robert Shaw.

2456. May 2, 1785 Lodowick Iseley, Henry Hart, Boston Garriner, & Adam Apple enter 159 ac in Guilford Co; border: George Summerman on E and Jacob Boon on S.

2457. May 7, 1785 John Sweet enters 75 ac in Guilford Co; border: on S side of Mary Beason, W side of John Hailey, & his own survey.

2458. May 16, 1785 Elisha Mendingall and Sarah Mash enter 200 ac in Guilford Co on waters of Hicory Cr; border: N corner of said Mash.

2459. May 16, 1785 Jacob Chrisman enters 200 ac in Guilford Co; border: on N by Redy fork, on W by widdow Grun's deeded land & "part" by Thomas Cummon's late survey or grant, on S "part by" Jacob Worick, & on E by his own 500 ac survey.

2460. May 17, 1785 John Robertson enters 50 ac in Guilford Co on waters of Haw R; border: William Robertson, Joseph Payn, & John Taylor's entry.

2461. May 17, 1785 William Bethel enters 80 ac in Guilford Co on waters of Lick fork Cr; border: Peter Lewis, the claimant, & Samuel Bethel.

page 65
2462. May 18, 1785 Jacob Crisman enters 167 ac in Guilford Co; border: on S by his former entry, on W by survey of Arthur Farbush, & on N by survey of James Chrestshlaw.

2463. May 19, 1785 Susannah Shoemaker enters 200 ac in Guilford Co on Haw R waters; border: deeded land of Jacob Summers, Boston Grainger, & Simmerman.

2464. May 21, 1785 Martha Tasey enters 250 ac in Guilford Co "a certain piece of land" entered by Alexander Tasey and caveated by James Johnson "agreeable to following verdict" vz. James Johnson to have 250 ac first without "hurting" Alexander Tasey's improvement; then Alexr Tasey to have 250 ac on S side of Moses McCaistions and Abraham Whitesides land.

2465. Jun. 1, 1785 William Parkhill enters 50 ac in Guilford Co on waters of Allimance Cr; border: Samuel McDill, William Cartary, & Charles Barney.

2466. Jun. 14, 1785 John Linder enters 400 ac in Guilford Co on Gumping Br a "drain" of Wolf Island Cr.

2467. Jun. 21, 1785 Adam Lackey enters 10 ac in Guilford Co on S Buffellow Cr waters; between claimants own deeded land & Charles Burney, John McBride, & George Donnel.

2468. Jul. 12, 1785 Ambrose Chappel enters 125 ac in Guilford Co on Rudduckses Cr; border: Rankin; includes his own improvement.
2469. Jul. 12, 1785 John Standley enters 200 ac in Guilford Co on branch of S Buffellow Cr; border: S of Michal Mason's corner.

2470. Jul. 22, 1785 (John Standley enters 200 ac in Guilford Co--lined out) William McGrady enters 40 ac in Guilford Co on waters of Brushy Cr; border: James McGrady, Thomas Thornberry, & Joseph Perkins.

2471. Jul. 25, 1785 James Henderson enters 195 ac in Guilford Co on head branch of second Rich fork; border: on E side of Isaac Liniger's entry, Joshua Hitchcock, & his land.

2472. Jul. 25, 1785 John Ritchey enters 106 ac in Guilford Co between N Buffelow Cr and Redy fork; border: Thomas Hamilton on S and John Lurkins on E.

2473. Jul. 30, 1785 Joseph Hoggatt enters 100 ac in Guilford Co on waters of Mordicais Cr; border: claimant's land where he lives.

2474. Jul. 30, 1785 James Gillaland enters 450 ac in Guilford Co on second Rich fork; border: on E side of Isaac Liniger's entry and his corner; includes Gilliland's improvement.

2475. Aug. 10, 1785 Edward Weatherley enters 100 ac in Guilford Co on waters of Redy fork; border: his own land, William Covey, & George Parks.

2476. Aug. 10, 1785 Jonas Ricks enters 200 ac in Guilford Co on waters of Mordicais Cr; border: Jonas Ricks' late survey and George Parks.

2477. Aug. 16, 1785 Andrew Carringer enters 159 ac in Guilford Co; border: Andrew Garinger's old survey on E and Adam Clapp's old deeded land on S.

page 67

2478. Aug. 16, 1785 John Waggoner enters 100 ac in Guilford Co; border: Adam Clapp's old deeded land, Andrew Garinger's on N, & John Waggoner's own land.

2479. Aug. 19, 1785 Adam Ritzel enters 115 ac in Guilford Co on waters of Stinkin Quarter Cr; near or border: Philip Kime and Peter Smith.

2480. Aug. 19, 1785 Thomas Hays enters 62 ac in Guilford Co on waters of Redy fork on Buckhorn Cr; border: on N of Nelson.

2481. Aug. 20, 1785 Isaac Cantrell enters 220 ac in Guilford Co on waters of Wolf Island Cr; border: John Linder and Laurance Bankston.

2482. Aug. 22, 1785 Turlton Johnson enters 640 ac in Guilford Co on waters of Deep R and Abbots Cr; border: John Haley on E and William Charles on S.

2483. Sept. 3, 1785 Robert Brattin enters 100 ac in Guilford Co on waters of Deep R; border: on W by William Reynolds, on S & E by David Worth, & N by Robert Lamb.

2484. Aug. 27, 1785 Philip Raddy (or Roddey) enters 100 ac in Guilford Co; border: his own survey where he lives.

2485. Oct. 10, 1785 John Cumming enters 50 ac in Guilford Co on waters of Jacobs Cr; border: his own deeded land.
2486. Oct. 11, 1785 Jesse Jones [enters] 105 ac in Guilford Co on Pole catt Cr waters of Deep R; border: Michael Wilson on E, survey of George Parks on S, & William Renolds on W.

2487. Oct. 12, 1785 Thomas Gosset enters 100 ac in Guilford Co on waters of Abets Cr; border: on N by Jas Henderson's entry and on W of Turlton Johnson's entry; includes improvement where Joseph Willson lives.

page 69
2488. Oct. 14, 1785 Michael Caffy enters 50 ac in Guilford Co on Long Br a "draught" of Jacobs Cr; border: E of Mullen and S of his own land.

2489. Oct. 17, 1785 Mary Hubbard enters 150 ac in Guilford Co on waters of and S side of Dann R; border: Jehu Martin (or Mostin), George Carter, James Roberts.

2490. Oct. 17, 1785 Sirus Lightfoot Roberts enters 150 ac in Guilford Co on waters of and N side of Dan R; border: John Minis, John Semon, & John May.

Guilford County, NC, Land Entries 1779-1796

2491. Nov. 10, 1785 John Daniel Carner enters in Guilford Co on waters of Jacobs Cr and Troublesom Cr; border: David Peeples and Moses Short.

2492. Nov. 12, 1785 Edward Wright enters 187.5 ac in Guilford Co in fork of N & S Buffellow Cr; border: Nathaniel Boyd desc, both sides of waggon road, Valintine Arnet, Joseph Brown, & Andrew Gray.

2493. Nov. 22, 1785 John Stevenson enters 200 ac in Guilford Co on waters of Allimance Cr; border: Jerih. Fields W line.

2494. Nov. 23, 1785 Peter Amack (or Amick) enters 100 ac in Guilford Co on waters of Stinking Quarter Cr; border: William Barnet; includes said Amack's improvement.

2495. Nov. 23, 1785 Smith Moore enters 300 ac in Guilford Co on waters of Deep R; border: on E side of John Hiett's deeded land.

2496. Nov. 26, 2785 Henry Colston enters 100 ac in Guilford Co on N side of Bever Island Cr on Rich Bottom Br; border: James Hunter and John Joyce.

2497. Dec. 5, 1785 Hezekiah Sanders enters 100 ac in Guilford Co; border: on S of Morgan's deeded land and S of his own [land].

page 69
2498. caveated by Nichl Larimer £4.17 paid. Jan. 17, 1786 Robert Gains enters 60 ac in Guilford Co on waters of Taffs alias Nicholas Larimers Cr; border: his own land, Nicholas Larimer, Isaac Whitworth, & Robert Gilliland.

2499. Jan. 17, 1786 Smith Rumley enters 139 ac in Guilford Co on waters of Redy fork; border: Edward Weatherley.

2500. Jan. 17, 1786 James Wright enters 200 ac in Guilford Co on waters of Redy fork; border: on both sides of main road, below James Boyd, Joshua Dean, John Maxwell, & Edward Weatherley.

2501. Jan. 19, 1785 Barnabas McCollum (or McCollm) enters 100 ac in Guilford Co on waters of Allimance Cr; border: James Dickey's N corner.

2502. Jan. 23, 1786 William Lane enters 300 ac in Guilford Co; border: Risdon Moore's S corner, John Hamilton, Joseph Hiett.

2503. Jan. 24, 1785 Richard Williams enters 120 ac in Guilford Co on waters of Ruddockses Cr; border: John Balinger and entry of Matthias Williams.

2504. Jan. 24, 1786 Barnet Waggoner enters 125 ac in Guilford Co on S side of Buffelow Cr; border: Nicholas Gift and Barnet Wagoner.

2505. Jan. 25, 1786 James Millis enters 80 ac in Guilford Co on waters of Hickory Cr and Pole cat Cr; border: Edward Miller's deeded land and Ralph Garrell's late survey.

2506. Jan. 26, 1786 George Mendenall enters 100 ac in Guilford Co on waters of Deep Cr; border: Smith Moore's late survey and Sarah Brasilton.

2507. Jan. 26, 1786 George Mendingall enters 200 ac in Guilford Co on both sides of Deep R; border: Hamilton's late survey and Smith Moore.

2508. Jan. 26, 1786 Peter Dent enters 200 ac in Guilford Co on head waters of Deep R; border: widow Hartgrove's improvement.

page 70
2509. Jan. 26, 1786 Elijah Stack enters 40 ac in Guilford Co on waters of S Buffaloe Cr; border: John McAdow's late entry.

2510. Jan. 27, 1786 Richard Moon enters 120 ac in Guilford Co on N & S side of Long Br that runs into Moons Cr; border: Richard Moon, Aaron Mendingall, Jacob Hunt, Austin Morris, & White.

2511. Jan. 27, 1786 William Montgomery enters 200 ac in Guilford Co on waters of Deep R; border: Stephen Gardner, Walton, Dennis Fome, & his own [land]; includes improvement formerly called Jackson's.

2512. Jan. 28, 1786 Jonathan Howel enters 75 ac in Guilford Co on waters of Deep R; border: on N & W by John Hamilton.

2513. Jan. 30, 1786 Stephen Brasilton Gardner enters 400 ac in Guilford Co on waters of Deep R on N side; border: John Hamilton, Isaac Holton.

2514. Jan. 30, 1786 Silas Williams enters 100 ac in Guilford Co on waters of S Buffaloe Cr; border: David Edwards, his own [land], & Samuel Frazer.

2515. Feb. 2, 1786 Williams Reynolds enters 500 ac in Guilford Co on waters of Hickory Cr and Pole catt Cr; border: his former entry on E & N.

2516. Feb. 3, 1786 William Linvill enters 100 ac in Guilford Co on waters of Reed Cr; border: Joseph Mimsum (or Munsum) and Robert Moore.

2517. Feb. 6, 1786 Richard Wallace enters 300 ac in Guilford Co on waters of Brush Cr; includes improvement where Orson Moore lives; border: Aaron Mendingall and Joseph Perkins.

2518. Feb. 6, 1786 William Dent enters 150 ac in Guilford Co on waters of Hogans Cr and Baleus Cr on both sides of main road; border: claim of Jesse Powers "purchased of" John Finley, Michael Henderson, & David Linvel.

page 72
2519. Feb. 21, 1786 Nathaniel McCommay enters 112 ac in Guilford Co on waters of Redy fork; border: on S of Joseph Jackson and on W of Nathaniel Simpson.

2520. Feb. 22, 1786 Zepheniah Tate enters 10 ac in Guilford Co; border: Haw R on S, his own land on N, & county line on E.

2521. Feb. 24, 1786 James Martin enters 300 ac in Guilford on waters of Deep R; border: Joseph Jeddings and Gardner's late survey; includes James Martin's improvement.

2522. Mar. 16, 1786 Edward Wright enters 105 ac in Guilford Co on N & S fork of Buffaloe Cr; border: John Gillaspie and Andrw. Gray.

2523. Mar. 25, 1786 Dennis Fowmy (or Fomey) enters 200 ac in Guilford Co in Springfield settlement on waters of Muddy Cr; border: Charles ODare desc, his improvement, Philip Roddy, Isaac Widows.

2524. Mar. 27, 1786 Philip Caple enters 150 ac in Guilford Co; border: Jno Waggoner and Jacob Boon.

2525. Mar. 28, 1786 Philip Kimes enters 50 ac in Guilford Co on waters of Little Stinkin Quarter Cr; border: his own deeded land where he lives.

2526. Mar (sic) 7, 1786 Rev David Caldwell enters 110 ac in Guilford Co on waters of Mordicais Cr; border: SE & SW corner of his entry #2272 and the county line.

2527. Mar. 22, 1786 (sic) Valintine Pegg enters 23 ac in Guilford Co on waters of Deep R; border: on S of Thomas Henderson's survey, on W of Moreland's survey, & N & E of John McCoy.

2528. Mar. 25, 1786 (sic) Garrard Stricker enters 100 ac in Guilford Co on waters of Rock Cr; border: Nicholas Gift, Henry Cobb, & claimant's land where he lives.

2529. Mar. 25, 1786 (sic) Robert Lindsey enters 100 ac in Guilford Co on waters of Deep R; border: William Webster, John McElroy, his own "plantation" where he lives, original deed granted to William Buis, Salisbury road, & his former entry.

page 72
2530. withdrawn and warrant returned. Apr. 25, 1786 Elisha Charles enters 25 ac in Guilford Co on waters of Deep R; border: Robert Lindsey's entry on the Great road, Samuel Hartgrove's deeded land, line of grant to William Buis, & includes his own land where he lives.

2531. May 9, 1786 Jacob Daniel Shearer enters 45 ac in Guilford Co on waters of Rock Cr; border: on two lines of Robert Pealey and claimant's late entry.

2532. May 13, 1786 William Shaver enters 12 ac in Guilford Co on waters of Rock Cr; border: tract of Robert Agnew and claimant's tract where he lives.

2533. May 18, 1786 Philip Borrow enters 300 ac in Guilford Co; border: Trother, Peter Smith, & the county line.

2534. May 19, 1786 Stephen Goff enters 200 ac in Guilford Co on waters of Redy fork; border: Patrick Diamond.

2535. May 19, 1786 Steward Diamond enters 60 ac in Guilford Co on N side of Redy fork of Haw R; border: William Gawdy esq, Patrick Diamond, & William Dickson.

2536. May 19, 1786 Joseph Faset enters 100 ac in Guilford Co on N side of Redy fork of Haw R; border: William Dickson, Patrick Diamond, & John Carnahan.

2537. May 31, 1786 John Howel enters 100 ac in Guilford Co on waters of Ruddocks Cr; border: Stephen Gardner & Isaac Gardner.

2538. Jun. 17, 1786 Daniel Dillon enters 50 ac in Guilford Co on waters of N Buffolow Cr; border: Alexr Braden, Joseph Ruckman, & Daniel Dortherty.

2539. Jul. 26, 1786 Robert Fields enters 185 ac in Guilford Co on Allimance Cr; border: his own land and Peter Fields.

2540. Aug. 17, 1786 Levi Coffin enters 40 ac in Guilford Co on dividing ridge between waters of N (& S--lined out) Buffelow Cr and waters of Horspen Cr; border: survey of Michael Mason, one of David Caldwell, and one of his own.

page 73

2541. Aug. 7, 1786 Andrew Findley enters 300 ac in Guilford Co on waters of Allemance Cr; border: said Finley (sic) on N & S.

2542. Aug. 7, 1786 Hugh Forbes (or Forbush) enters 500 ac in Guilford Co on waters of Buffolow Cr; border: Kerr on W and Jacob Stricklain on N.

2543. Aug. 22, 1786 Caleb Story enters 50 ac in Guilford Co on Millstone Br; border: Martin Pegg and Thomas Henderson.

2544. Aug. 29, 1786 John Hitton enters 200 ac in Guilford Co on branch of Rich fork of Abbits Cr; border or near: Joseph Tomlinson, Henry Pitts, & ridge road.

2545. Sept. 6, 1786 John Talbot enters 296 ac in Guilford Co on waters of Deep R; border: William Gardner, Christopher Heatt jr, Samuel Frazier, & Rubin Bunker.

2546. Sept. 15, 1786 John Hawkins enters 50 ac in Guilford Co on Beaver Cr; border: Tobias Clap, John Foust, Elisha Bennit, & his own land.

2547. Sept. 22, 1786 Tarlton Johnson enters 150 ac in Guilford Co on waters of Abbots Cr; border: James Henderson on W and his own land on N.

2548. Nov. 8, 1786 Joshua Hedgcock enters 112 ac in Guilford Co on Dry fork of Abbots Cr; border: his old entry.

2549. Nov. 16, 1786 Thomas Greddlebough enters 100 ac in Guilford Co on waters of Hicrick fork; border: Joshua Hitchcock, Guilford County line, & John Hitchcock; includes his own improvement.

2550. Nov. 21, 1786 John Hood enters 200 ac in Guilford Co on S side of S Buffolow Cr; border: Thos Morgan's NW corner.
2551. Nov. 23, 1786 William Burney enters 50 ac in Guilford Co; border: John Anderson's N line and John Larkin's E & W line.

2552. Nov. 29, 1786 Richard Whaley enters 90 ac in Guilford Co on waters of Hicory Cr; border: Bradford on N, Joseph Swean on S, WIlliam Wagon on W, & Edward Mills on E.

2553. Dec. 7, 1786 Robert Pierce enters 85 ac in Guilford Co; border: Thomas Rue and Thimothey Barnet.

page 74

2554. Dec. 23, 1786 John Larkin enters 50 ac in Guilford Co on waters of N Buffaloe & Reedy fork; border: claimant's land and widow Caswell's land where she lives.

2555. Dec. 25, 1786 William Burney enters 100 ac in Guilford Co; border: John Anderson's N line and John Larkin's E & W line.

2556. withdrawn money returned. Jan. 1, 1787 Micaijah Terrell enters 400 ac in Guilford Co; between Jesse Williams, John Stanley, Frazer, Asa Hunt, Silas Williams, & George Hyatt.

2557. Jan. 18, 1787 Elizabeth Forbes (or Forbush) enters 200 ac in Guilford Co on waters of Blackwood Cr; between Jacob Strickling and William Montgomery sr.

2558. Jan. 18, 1787 Samuel Hunter enters 100 ac in Guilford Co on waters of Stinkin Quarter Cr; border: Robert Adams.

2559. Jan. 25, 1787 Stephen Scissna enters 50 ac in Guilford Co on waters of Brush Cr; border: Charles Bruce esq and land where Thos Wright now lives.

2560. Feb. 9, 1787 Joseph Canaday enters 125 ac in Guilford Co on Beaver Cr; border: his own land on N, Andrew Gambol on W, and widow Gayby & John Brigam on S.

2561. Feb. 19, 1787 Georg Forbes (or Forbush) enters 100 ac in Guilford Co on waters of Birch Cr a "draught" of Allemance Cr; border: Thomas Morgan & Andrew Shirk.

2562. Feb. 20, 1787 Jacob Nutt enters 50 ac in Guilford Co on waters of Great Allamance Cr; border: on N by Samuel Tucker, on E by Dobsin & Allexander, on S by William Dickies, & on W by his own [land].

2563. Feb. 22, 1787 Watson Warton enters 55 ac; border: on N by Taylor, on E by John Gilbert, on N by N Buffaloe Cr, & on W by claimant's own land.

2564. Mar. 8, 1787 Hance Cosby (or Crosby) enters 150 ac in Guilford Co on waters of Allamance Cr; border: Matthias Amuk on E, John Beaeley on N, & John McBride on W.

2565. Mar. 27, 1787 John McKaige enters 200 ac in Guilford Co on waters of Great Allamance Cr; border: on E by Michael Shitterling and on N by Fredrick Craft.

page 75

2566. Mar. 30, 1787 John McAdow enters 30 ac in Guilford Co on S side of Buffaloe Cr; border: William Milun and George Pope.

2567. Mar. 31, 1787 James Coots enters 80 ac in Guilford Co on waters of Reedy fork; border: James Brown's SW corner.

2568. Apr. 3, 1787 John P Smith enters 30 ac in Guilford Co on waters of Stinking Water Cr; border: George Wiker, Peter Amos, & his own land.

2569. Apr. 6, 1787 James Ryan enters 200 ac in Guilford Co in Springfield settlement on waters of Muddy fork; border: on E by Dimis Towmy and the county line.

2570. Apr. 12, 1787 James Martin enters 188 ac in Guilford Co on waters of Deep R; border: on W of late survey of said Martin.

2571. Apr. 13, 1787 Joseph Massey enters 240 ac in Guilford Co; border: William Hoggatt's NE corner, county line, & William Fields.

2572. Apr. 23, 1787 Solomon Reynolds enters 100 ac in Guilford Co on waters of Hickory Cr; border: Jno McAdow and Wm Reynolds; includes improvement made by Thos Williams.

2573. Apr. 23, 1787 Stephen Gough (or Goff) enters 60 ac in Guilford Co on waters of Haw R; border: on S by his late survey, on N by Willm Dixon, & on W by Jno Campbel.

2574. __?__ due withdrawn. Apr. 30, 1787 James Wheatley enters 200 ac in Guilford Co on waters of Horse pinn Cr; border: on NW of William Brittain's deeded land and Thos Thombury's deeded land; includes improvement he lives on and improvement he formerly lived on.

2575. May 7, 1787 Daniel McMin enters 135 ac in Guilford Co in fork of Bever Cr; border: on E by William Shaw, on N by Jno Forbes, & on W by Joseph Canady.

2576. May 28, 1787 John Leonard enters 450 ac in Guilford Co on waters of Pole cat Cr; border: Daniel Shearwood and widow Swam; includes his own improvement.

2577. caveated by Jno McBride. May 23, 1787 Andrew Russell enters 60 ac in Guilford Co on waters of S Buffaloe Cr; border: on SW corner of John McAdow's entry.

2578. May 24, 1787 Thomas Finley enters 200 ac in Guilford Co on "great waters" of Allamance Cr; border: Robert Merrew's (or Menew) "plantation" on S and Jeremiah Fields on W.

page 76
2579. Jun. 6, 1787 Mary Hawkins enters 300 ac in Guilford Co on waters of Beaver Cr; border: Tobias Clap, Isaac Grason, said "Hawkings", & Daniel May.

2580. Aug. 3, 1787 Jarrald Burrow enters 135 ac in Guilford Co on waters of Stinkin Quarter Cr; border: Orange County line, tract called Trotter's land, & land where claimant lives.

2581. Jun. 11, 1787 Daniel Dillon jr enters 100 ac in Guilford Co; border: Massey on W, Ballinger on E, & "perhaps" on waters of Reddocks Cr.

2582. withdrawn warrant to be taken in. Jun. 14, 1787 Anthony Sharpe enters 640 ac in Guilford Co on waters of & both sides of Hickory Cr; border: formerly Mendingall's land; includes the copper mines and improvement where Healy lived.
2583. withdrawn. Jun. 14, 1787 Anthony Sharpe enters 640 ac in Guilford Co on both sides of Hickory Cr; border: his own entry and others.

2584. withdrawn. Jun. 14, 1787 Anthony Sharpe enters 250 ac on waters of big Allamance Cr; border: on E side of Samuel Devenney, on W [of] John Copelin's deeded land, on S of Robert Fields, on N of Edward Long on both sides of Quaker Road.

2585. withdrawn. Jun. 14, 1787 Anthony Sharpe enters 150 ac in Guilford Co; border: on S side of Jeremiah Shelley's land taken by Bennett Bradford and E of John Healey where "he" lives.

2586. withdrawn. Jun. 14, 1787 Anthony Sharpe enters 150 ac in Guilford Co on waters of Allamance and Bever Creeks; border: Henry Whitsel's survey, Jacob Sools, & Matthias Sevings.

2587. withdrawn. Jun. 14, 1787 Anthony Sharpe enters 150 ac in Guilford Co; border: on S side of John Healy where Isaac Widdows lives, on W of Jeremiah Shelly's taken by Bennett Bradford, & on N side of Jno Healey's deeded land.

2588. Jun. 23, 1787 James Maxwell enters 36 ac in Guilford Co on waters of Haw R; border: deeded land pf Joshua Deen and Samuel Faris.

page 77

2589. Sept. 8, 1787 Silvanus Gardner enters 60 ac in Guilford Co on waters of Beavers Cr; border: on E by Thomas Taylor (or Tayllr), on S by Drury Watson, & on N by John Cummins.

2590. Sept. 25, 1787 George Forbis (or Forbush) enters 40 ac in Guilford Co on waters of Buffaloe Cr; border: N of his own old survey.

2591. Oct. 3, 1787 Joel Sanders enters 200 ac in Guilford Co on waters of Deep R; border: Richard Bull, Joseph Iddms and Samuel Lamb.

2592. "William Dillon". Oct. 13, 1787 William McAlhatan enters 50 ac in Guilford Co on waters of Reedy fork; border: James McCuishim's old deeded land on W and Arthur Forbes.

2593. Oct. 26, 1787 John Coots enters 100 ac in Guilford Co on S side of & adjoining Reedy fork of Haw R; border: on N side of tract where Gilerel lives.

2594. Oct. 3, 1787 Richard Ozment sr enters 50 ac in Guilford Co on S side of Stoney Cr; border: John Hunter, Florence Sullivan, Josiah Trotter, & Francis Cummings.

2595. Nov. 2, 1787 Robert Thompson enters 100 ac in Guilford Co on S side of Reedy fork; border: John McClintock on E and Reedy fork on N.

page 78 (blank page)

page 79   "Entries made by Alexander McKeen esq, entry taker of Guilford Co, commencing Nov. court 1787."
2596. Dec. 24, 1787 Owen Lane enters 40 ac in Guilford Co on waters of S Buffolo Cr; border: Parks' old place on N, by Gorrel on E, Lovet on S, & Martin on W.

2597. Dec. 24, 1787 Hance Hamilton enters 50 ac in Guilford Co on waters of Redy fork; border: said Hamilton and Henry Ross.
2598. Feb. 7, 1788 Daniel Shurwood enters 80 ac in Guilford Co on waters of Alimance Cr; border: Jno Stewart on E, on S by Stewart's claim, on W by Wm Kelly, & on N by Aaron Manship.

2599. Feb. 18, 1788 John Hall enters 10 ac in Guilford Co on waters of S Buffolo Cr; border: Ralph Gorell, John Orr, his own land, & John Foster; includes a small improvement.

2600. Mar. 29, 1788 John McAdow enters 50 ac in Guilford Co on waters of S Buffalow Cr; border: George Parks' E corner.

2601. transfered to Jonathan Armfield. Mar. 29, 1788 John McBride enters 50 ac in Guilford Co on waters of Hicory Cr; border: Bradford's old tract and James McCuistion.

2602. May 2, 1788 Adam Mitchel sr enters 200 ac in Guilford Co on branch of waters of N Buffelow Cr; border: land where claimant lives.

2603. May 19, 1788 Joseph Truet enters 10 ac in Guilford Co on waters of Haw R; border: on SW corner of claimant's land he bought from Robert Tedford.

2604. May 20, 1788 David Hodson enters 107 ac in Guilford Co on waters of Pole cat Cr; border: Sury Moses and Ralph Gorrel.

2605. Jun. 11, 1788 James Warnock enters 50 ac in Guilford on S side of Haw R; border: his own [land] and David Mackin's deeded land.

2606. Aug. 16, 1788 Benjamin Merrel enters 212 ac in Guilford Co on waters of Rich fork of Abets Cr; border: Jas Gillaland and Moses Mendinghall.

2607. Aug. 21, 1788 Ralph Gorrel enters 40 ac in Guilford Co on waters of Pole cat Cr; border: surveyed and deeded land of Daniel Shearwood, John Johnson, & Leonard.

page 80
2608 Aug. 21, 1788 James McAdow enters 37 ac in Guilford Co on waters of Allimance Cr; border: Wm Cusick, Francis McBride, Wm Donnell, & the claimant.

2609. Aug. 22, 1788 Elisabeth Scott, widow, enters 80 ac in Guilford Co on S side of Haw R; border: tract said widow lives on, a branch, & Joshua Underwood.

2610. Sept. 23, 1788 James Thompson enters 120 ac in Guilford Co on waters of Hicory Cr; border: John Ozburn sr and John Lowder.

2611. Oct. 1, 1788 George Chrisman enters 20 ac and 64 poles in Guilford Co on waters of Travises Cr; border: Peter Summer and the county line.

2612. Oct. 1, 1788 Christian Fall enters 160 ac in Guilfrod Co on S side of Branch of Travises Cr; border: claimant's land, John Trolinger, Daniel Winigh.

2613. Oct. 8, 1788 John Stephenson enters 40 ac in Guilford Co on waters of Allimance Cr; border: Mathew Stevenson on N and Wm Dobson on S.

2614. Oct. 10, 1788 Abner Weatherley enters 60 ac in Guilford Co; border: on W by David Love, on S by Abner Weatherly, and E & N by Samuel Fulten (or Futton).

2615. caveated by John Rankin. Oct. 13, 1788 Abraham McElhatten enters 5 ac in Guilford Co; border: John Nicks' NW corner and John Rankin.

2616. Oct. 14, 1788 Daniel McMin enters 150 ac in Guilford Co on Bever Cr; border: on E by William Shaw, on N by "my own", & on W by James Kirkman and James Ramley.

2617. Nov. 19, 1788 John Osic enters 50 ac in Guilford Co on both sides of Ridg fork; border: Henry Hart on N, claimant's [land] on NW, Wm Summers on S, & Andr Smith on E.

2618. Nov. 19, 1788 Daniel May jr enters 150 ac in Guilford Co on waters of big Allimance Cr; border: Daniell May sr, Tobias Clap on N, & Ralph Gorrel on E.

2619. Dec. 5, 1788 Wm Helton enters 100 ac in Guilford Co on waters of Deep R; border: W corner of James Helton.

page 81
2620. Dec. 8, 1788 Mordica Mendinghall enters 418 ac in Guilford Co on S fork of Deep R; border: on N side of Wm Tumbleston, Charles Odar, & Philip Rody.

2621. Dec. 9, 1788 Volintine Mileham enters 120 (write over) ac in Guilford Co on waters of Redy fork; border: James Work's E & W line, on E by Samuel Mileham, & land of John Meek desc.

2622. Dec. 26, 1788 John Haley and John Hamilton enter 300 ac "in partnership" in Guilford Co on both sides of Deep R; border: John Mendinghall on E "now entered" John Shelley on N, Smith Moore on W, & George (Mendinghall--lined out) Manliffon on S.

2623. Dec. 26, 1788 Martha Tasey enters 200 ac in Guilford Co on N side of Redy fork; border: James White, John White desc, William Gowdy, & Abraham Whitesides.

2624. Dec. 26, 1788 Thomas Archer enters 30 ac in Guilford Co on waters of Deep R; border: NW corner of "my" own deeded land.

2625. Dec. 27, 1788 Thomas Archer enters 20 ac in Guilford Co on waters of Deep R; border: his own land and John Unthank.

2626. Jan. 8, 1789 John Gildchrist (sic) and John McClintock enters 300 ac in Guilford Co on S side of Redy fork of Haw R and waters thereof; border: land where John Gilchrist lives and on W by land where John John (sic) McClintock lives.

2627. Jan. 10, 1789 Leven Williams enters 250 ac in Guilford Co; includes his own improvement on waters of Bull Run; border: Wm Williams' SW corner.

2628. Jan. 13, 1789 Thomas Crouch enters 50 ac in Guilford Co on N side of S Buffelow Cr; border: Samuel Everet, Ralph Gorrel, & William Mebin.

page 82
2629. Jan. 19, 1789 George Kirkman "locates" 9.5 ac in Guilford Co on waters of Poal cat Cr; border: Daniel Suliven, Elijah Manship, & claimant's land.

2630. Jan. 24, 1789 Jonathan Hodson "locates" 76 ac in Guilford Co on waters of Pole cat Cr; border: Sarah Mash and David Hodson.

2631. Jan. 27, 1789 Hartwell Barham enters 74 (write over) ac in Guilford Co on waters of Mars fork; border: Archibald McMical, Peter Harris, & his own land.

2632. Jan. 28, 1789 Robt Thompson enters 100 ac in Guilford Co on S side of Redy fork of Haw R; border: deeded land [of] John Gilchrist on W.

2633. Feb. 6, 1789 Peter Rian Simpson enters 122 ac in Guilford Co on waters of Redy fork; border: John Mecks desc SE corner and Wm Dickson.

2634. Feb. 13, 1789 Hance Hamilton, John H Spruce, & John Hamilton "in partnership" enter 50 ac in Guilford Co on waters of S Buffelow Cr; between David Kerr sr, David Kerr jr, & John Hood.

2635. Feb. 16, 1789 "for" William Dickey [enters] 90 ac; border: Robert Neley and Thomas McCullock.

2636. Feb. 25, 1789 Charles Bruce enters 12 ac on waters of Redy fork in Guilford Co; border: John Robinson, Humphrey Loid, Archabald McMical, & claimant's own land.

2637. "drawn". Apr. 6, 1789 Daniel Sullivan (or Salivan) enters 100 ac on waters of Polcat Cr; border: NW corner of William Kelley's late survey, George Kirkman, & John Stewart.

2638. Apr. 8, 1789 John Forbush enters 125 ac in Guilford Co on waters of Burch Cr; border: on E side of his own land.

page 86
2639. May 8, 1789 William Montgomery enters 45 ac; border: on S by McGamcery, on W by McClintoch, on N by Gillchrist, & on E by his own land.

2640. May 25, 1789 John Wolfington enters 150 ac in Guilford Co; border: widow Kersey on N, land formerly belonging to John Sanders on E, & land where Willm Grier formerly lived.

2641. May 25, 1789 Mordaica Lane enters 100 ac on waters of Deep R; border: George Mendinghall "known formerly by" Calebb Blagg's entry.

2642. Jun. 6, 1789 Simon Moon enters 112 ac in Guilford Co on waters of Reedy fork of Haw R; border: Daniel Dillon's old line and Nathan Dillon; includes his own improvement where he lives.

2643. Jul. 14, 1789 Jul. 14, 1789 Henry Whitsel enters 60 ac in Guilford Co on waters of Allimance Cr; border: Sampson Powel, Matthias Swing, & claimant's land.

2644. Aug. 12, 1789 Christian Fall enters 350 ac in Guilford Co on prong of Harris' Cr; border: Summers' deeded land, Jacob Crisman, & claimant's land.

2645. Aug. 18, 1789 William Wart enters 50 ac on waters of Deep R; border: Tailton Johnson and Robert Burnett.

2646. Aug. 23, 1789 Thomas Harper [enters] 212.5 ac in Guilford Co on Rich fork waters; border: Joshua & John Hichcok and Fileman Cuddleborough.

page 84
2647. Sept. 4, 1789 Joseph Stanley enters 60 ac in Guilford Co on waters of Reedy fork; border: Joel Sanders and Simon Moon.

2648. Dec. 1, 1789 John Gillaspie enters 150 ac in Guilford Co on waters of S Buffaloe Cr; border: "my" own corner, Mr. Kerr, & Jesse Weatherly.

2649. Dec. 14, 1789 Abagail Wilson enters 200 ac in Guilford Co on waters of Pole catt Cr; border: Michael Wilson, Jacob Jones, & claimant's land.

2650. withdrawn, Dec. 22, 1789 John Shaw enters 200 ac in Guilford Co; border: John Hiatt, John Mendingall, John McCurrey, & John Benson.

2651. Dec. 24, 1789 George Hamilton enters 60 ac in Guilford Co on waters of Buffaloe Cr; border: Charles Bruce's N & S line, George Wilson, his line, & Robt Marley.

2652. "returns made up to this date". Dec. 28, 1789 Stephen Sisney enters 60 ac in Guilford Co on waters of Horspen Cr; border: on NW of William Brittain's deeded land and Thos Thornborough's deeded land; includes improvement "he now in possession of".

2653. Jan. 14, 1790 James Wolfington enters 200 ac in Guilford Co on waters of Mordaicais Cr; border: Isaac Widow, John Wolfington, & David Caldwell.

page 85
2654. Jan. 18, 1790 William Diamond enters 100 ac on waters of Redy fork of Haw R; border: on E by William Russel, on W by John Hays, on N by Patrick Diamond, & on S by Martha Erwin.

2655. Feb. 15, 1790 Thomas Plunket enters 30 ac in Guilford Co on waters of Stinking Quarter Cr; border: land said Thomas Plunket "got by his wife" and Hawkins.

2656. Feb. 15, 1790 Christian Iseley (or July) enters 15 ac in Guilford Co on waters of Buck Cr; border: Wm Shaver, Lodwick Whitsll, Lodwick Iseley, & claimant.

2657. Feb. 16, 1790 Lodwick Clap enters 50 ac in Guilford Co on waters of Bever Cr; border: Tobias Clap on E and claimant on W.

2658. Feb. 17, 1790 James Walker enters 300 ac; border: Henry Hustes McCullock's old boundary line, Robert Morrow's N & S line, & "above entry drawn".

2659. warrant for this entry to be issued to James Gilleland by order of both "entrors". Feb. 28, 1790 J Hamilton and J Haley enter 250 ac in Guilford Co on waters of Abots Cr; border: Isaac Linagar and James Gilleland.

2660. Mar. 5, 1790 Thomas Donnel Lett enters 60 ac in Guilford Co on waters of big Allemance Cr; border: Shederick Dean, "his" line, & Findley Stewart.

2661. Mar. 8, 1790 George May enters 100 ac in Guilford Co; border: Samuel Low, John Cook, & John Hawkins.

page 86
2662. Mar. 9, 1790 James Brown enters 50 ac in Guilford Co on waters of Danels Cr; border: Danill Ozburn on N and William Ozburn on S.

2663. Mar. 9, 1790 James Gardner enters 50 ac; border: Samuel Fulton on E, his own deeded land on S, & George Brown on W.

2664. Mar. 10, 1790 John Ozeas (or Orie) enters on Crooked Br; border: on E by Daniel Apple, on E of George Lowdela, on S of Thomas Sexton, & on W of Philip Rhodes.

2665. Mar. 30, 1790 John Hodson enters 85 ac in Guilford Co on waters of Pole cat Cr; border: George Kirkman and David Jones.

2666. May 7, 1790 George Mendinghall enters 50 ac; border: John Brazilton on N side; "above entry drawn".

2667. May 7, 1790 George Mendinghall enters 250 ac on waters of Deep R; border: Stephen Gardner on E side and John Hawel on W side; "above entry drawn".

2668. May 10, 1790 Benjamin Sermon enters 200 ac on waters of Allimance on Brushley fork; border: Jeremiah Fild (sic), William Field, Robert Field, Peter Field, & Thomas Cawsey.

2669. caveated by Abagail Ozburn Aug, 2. May 15, 1790 Jesse Lane enters 100 ac in Guilford Co; border: Joseph Ozburn and waters of David's Cr.

2670. May 17, 1790 John Nelson enters 50 ac on Buckhorn Cr waters of Reedy fork; border: on N side of Nelson's line.

page 87
2671. May 28, 1790 Philip Lodwick enters 190 ac in Guilford Co on "South waters" of Reedy fork of Haw R; border: "my" own deeded land on E, Henry Herd on S, John Trolinger on W, Christian Fall on S, & claim of Cloll Lam on S; includes "my" improvement "in part".

2672. Jun. 12, 1790 The "Calvin & Lutherin" congregations living in Guilford Co on waters of Travises Cr, jointly and for use of each other and benefit of building a house or house of worship there on, enter 10 ac in Guilford Co;

border: on N & W by Basten Garinger and on E by widow Shoemaker; includes a meeting house and school house.

2673. Jun. 12, 1790 Calvin & Lutherin congregations living on waters of Travises Cr, jointly and for the use of each other for benefit of building and erecting a house or houses of worship thereon, enter 70 ac in Guilford Co; border: on W by Daniel Wanick, on N by Philip Lodwick, on E by Christian Fall, & on S by Jacob Christman; includes "the" house and spring.

2674. Jun. 15, 1790 William May enters 50 ac in Guilford Co on waters of Hickory Cr; border: on E side of his own entry.

2675. Jul. 19, 1790 Jonathan Wilson enters 50 ac in Guilford Co on waters of Deep R; border: John Stafford, Allexander Forguson, George Jamison, & his own land.

2676. Jun. 28, 1790 Robert Burmjet (or Burnet) enters 100 ac in Guilford Co; border: John Healey, Smith Moore, & Thomas Busis.

2677. Jul. 10, 1790 John Hyatt enters 50 ac in Guilford Co on waters of Izeal Cr; border: SW corner of "my" own old deeded land.

page 88
2678. Aug. 2, 1790 William Way enters 100 ac in Guilford Co on waters of Daniel Ozburns Cr; border: Solomon Reynells.

2679. Aug. 16, 1790 George Mendingall enters 128 ac in Guilford Co on waters of Deep R; border: James Deming.

2680. Aug. 17, 1790 John Stewart enters 100 ac in Guilford Co on waters of Pole cat Cr; border: his own [land] and Farigail.

2681. Aug. 17, 1790 Benjamin Barnett enters 6 ac; border: at N end of his land and Richard Ozburn.

2682. Aug. 19, 1780 Daniel Lane enters 50 ac in Guilford Co; border: Benbow on E side.

2683. Sept. 3, 1790 Samuel Casey enters 50 ac in Guilford Co; border: Thos Morgan, Willm Peasley, & John McMullin.

2684. Sept. 6, 1790 John Swing enters 40 ac in Guilford Co on waters of Bever Cr; border: Matthias Swing, Jacob CLapp, & Jacob Suit.

2685. "this entry is drawn not returned from 2652". Oct. 23, 1790 James Criswell enters 10 ac in Guilford Co on N side of Reedy fork and waters thereof; border: deeded land of Robert Thompson and claimant.

2686. Dec. 28, 1790 Samuel Diving (or Diviney) enters 300 ac in Guilford Co on waters of Sandy Cr and Stinking Quarter Cr; border: his own former survey.

2687. Jan. 10, 1791 John Gillaspie enters 100 ac in Guilford Co on waters of S Buffaloe Cr; border: George Duskey's SW corner.

page 89
2688. Jan. 17, 1791 Joseph Stanley enters 60 ac in Guilford Co on waters of Reedy fork; border: claimant's land, Joel Sanders, & Benjamin Brittian.

2689. Feb. 17, 1791 Matthew Coffin enters 200 ac in Guilford Co; border: "my" own land on E, James Gilleland on W, Talton Johnston on N, & Richard Dayson on S.

2690. Feb. 22, 1791 Robert Morrow enters 33 ac in Guilford Co on waters of Allamance Cr; border: widow Hawkins.

2691. Feb. 23, 1791 George Cortner enters 190 ac in Guilford Co; border: Matthias Emick on N on Allimance Cr waters, Col. John Peasley on SE side, Conrod Haga on S, & Matthias Swing on W.

2692. Mar. 5, 1791 Ezekiel Duvcast (or Duest) enters 80 ac in Guilford Co on waters of Reedy fork of Haw R; border: Valintine Mileham, William Gowdy, RObert Russell, Nathaniel Simpson, & Ezekiel Deweace.

2693. Mar. 7, 1791 Andrew Carmichael enters 100 ac in Guilford Co on waters of Brushy fork; border: John Dobson's W line, Josephs Mauis, & William Gorrel.

2694. Mar. 10, 1791 Stephen Gough (or Goff) enters 40 ac in Guilford Co; border: Walter Mileham, Peter Byan Simson, & William Dixon.

2695. Mar. 14, 1791 Peter Smith enters 100 ac in Guilford Co; border: Philip Crines, Adam Ritsel, county line, David Thornburg, & Peter Smith.

2696. Mar. 31, 1791 Adam Wright enters 15 ac in Guilford Co on waters of Little Stinking Quarter Cr; border: claimant's land and Uriah Springer.

2697. Apr. 2, 1791 Stephen Grough (or Goff) enters 40 ac in Guilford Co; border: Henry Billingsley, William Gowdy, & William Diamond.

2698. Apr. 24, 1791 Joseph Unthark enters 31 ac in Guilford Co; border: land where claimant's monther lives and John Rankin.

2699. Jun. 1, 1791 Peter Field enters 50 ac in Guilford Co on waters of Allimance Cr; border: Jeremiah Fields and land "onse" owned by Joseph Field.

2700. Jun. 25, 1791 Philip Hoggatt enters 100 ac in Guilford Co on waters of Brush Cr; border: Robert Gallbraith, Arnold Hoskin, his old deeded land, James Thoras, & Benjamin Johnson.

2701. Aug. 27, 1791 Elias Cowin enters 200 ac in Guilford Co on waters of Allimance Cr; border: Thomas Bignm, Elias Cowin, & David Cowper.

2702. Aug. 27, 1791 John H Spruce enters 140 ac in Guilford Co on waters of S Buffaloe Cr; border: Hugh Forbes, David Kerr's deeded land, Saml Casey, & John McMullin.

2703. caveated by Samuel Low; entry and caveat both drawn. Sept. 8, 1791 Isaac Greson enters 30 ac in Guilford Co; between his own land and Samuel Low; border: David Low.

page 91
2704. Sept. 29, 1791 Elisha Bennett enters 100 ac in Guilford Co on waters of Stinking Quarter Cr; border: Saml Low, Willm Plunkett, George Gloss, & David Low.

2705. Nov. 11, 1791 Goerge Mendingall enters 75 ac in Guilford Co on waters of Richland Cr; border: Greer, Thomas Bullar, & William Montgomery's survey.

2706. Nov. 11, 1791 James Edwards enters 150 ac in Guilford Co on waters of N Buffaloe Cr; border: Silas Williams, William Edwards, David Edwards, & Paul May.

page 92 [blank page]
page 93 "Entries made by John Starrat esq, entry taker of Guilford Co; AD 1792 commencing Feby court."
2707 (1). no land for this entry to cover warrants; released(?) on oath of surveyor & money returned. Mar. 12, 1792 John McMurry enters 100 ac in Guilford Co on waters of N Buffaloe Cr; border: on E by land of orphans of William Anderson desc, on N by McKnight, & on S by Mitchel.

2708 (2). Apr. 16, 1792 David Louh sr enters 18 ac in Guilford Co on waters of Great Allemance Cr; border: George Clap, old Nicott (or Nuott), & a new survey of Thomas Plunket "being of a triangular figure".

2709 (3). May 3, 1792 John Spruce enters 200 ac in Guilford Co on both sides of Muddy Br of N Buffaloe Cr; border: John Nicks, William Spruce, Nathal. Boyd's entry, & Thomas Charles Craft's entry.

2710 (4). 180 ac of this entry is disputed & money returned on oath of surveyor. May 15, 1792 THomas Charles Craft enters 333 (written over 300) ac in Guilford Co on waters of N & S Buffaloe Creeks; border: on N side of one of said Craft's own entrys and S side of other of said Craft's entrys; includes remainder of his improvement.

2711 (5). May 24, 1792 John Higot enters 50 ac in Guilford Co on waters of Russells Run; border: Benjamin Smith(?), Mary Holland, & said Hignot.

2712 (6). May 24, 1792 Allen Willson enters 150 ac in Guilford Co on waters of Pole cat Cr; border: Abagail Willson's W line and Wm Reynolds (desc?).

2713 (7). May 24, 1792 Eli A Driskil (or Kuskel) enters of Guilford Co on waters of Buffaloe Cr; border: Col. Gullaspie on W and entry of Thos Charles Craft on E.

2714 (8). Jul. 2, 1792 Christian Farmer enters 40 ac in Guilford Co on waters of Allimance Cr; border: on N by Col. Peasley and on E by Conrade Hackey.

page 94
2715 (9). Jul. 16, 1792 Thomas Stokes enters 30 ac in Guilford Co on waters of Reedy fork of Haw R; border: on S by John Walker, on W by Nathan Gladson, on N by Joshua Dun, & on E by said Stokes.

2716 (10). Jul. 16, 1792 Charles Norman enters 40 ac in Guilford Co on waters of Bonejai Cr waters of Haw R; border: John Chilcart on N, Joshua Dun on E, & Edward Weatherley on S.

2717 (11). Jul. 21, 1792 Jenkin Sullivan enters 75 ac in Guilford Co on waters of Stinking Quarter Cr; border: Philip Barrow and Sullivand's old entry.

2718 (12). Aug. 12, 1792 Solomon Grace enters 100 ac in Guilford Co on waters of Stinkin Quarter Cr; border: on N by Jenkin Sullivan's late entry, survey of said Grace on W, & by another survey of said Grace on E; includes part of his improvement.

2719 (13). Aug. 15, 1792 Nathaniel Grace enters 100 ac in Guilford Co on waters of Stinking Quarter Cr; border: on S corner of tract called "Aggelon" and Randolph [County] line.

2720 (14). Aug. 20, 1792 William Jarrell enters 80 ac in Guilford Co on waters of Stinking Quarter Cr; border: Charles Wardin and Peter Field.

2721 (15). Elijah Dawson relinquished his right of this entry to Jetho New; issued in name of Jetho New & Jethro New relinquished his right of entry to Aaron Dishorn(?) and warrant issued. Nov. 22, 1792 Elijah Dawson enters 40 ac in Guilford Co on waters of Haw R; border: on W side of Ross, On S by Jethro New, on W by Jackson, & N by said Dawson.

2722 (16). Dec. 16, 1792 Joseph Rumbley enters 106 ac in Guilford Co on waters of Rock Run of Allimance Cr; border: on E by Andrew Law, on S by Thomas Hopkins, & Betty Muirs on W.

page 95
2723 (17). Dec. 17, 1792 David Jones enters 100 ac in Guilford Co on waters of Pole Cat Cr; border: Abigal Wilson, John Hodgin, Martin, & Isaac Jones.
2724 (18). no land to be found; entry withdrawn & money returned to claimant. Dec. 20, 1792 Solomon Grace enters 50 ac in Guilford Co on waters of Stinking Quarter Cr; part of land he bought from Matthew Hamilton.

2725 (19). Dec. 22, 1792 Abraham Gosset enters 200 ac in Guilford Co on waters of Deep R; border: county line, Elisha Mendingall, John Walton, & Randolph [County] line.

2726 (20). Jan. 21, 1793 Christian Fall enters 6 ac in Guilford Co on waters of Redy fork; border: on E "part" by Abner Weatherley & Martin Wyrick, Samuel Fulton on N, on W by "despected" land, & on S by his own land.

2727 (21). Feb. 15, 1793 Matthew Coffin enters 150 ac in Guilford Co on waters of Rich fork of Abots Cr; border: on N by John Hitcock and on W by John McCurry & Burnet.

2728 (22). Feb. 15, 1793 Patrick McGibbony (or McGibeney), in behalf of heirs of Henry Work, enters 50 ac in Guilford Co on waters of Haw R; border: on N & W by Henry Work's land and on E by James Work.

2729 (23). Feb. 22, 1793 George Hiatt jr enters 40 ac in Guilford Co on waters of Deep R; border: on S by Meshuk Couch, on W by Matthew Mays, his own land, Christopher Hietts on N, & Henry Camplin on E.

2730 (24). Feb. 24, 1793 John Hubbard enters 60 ac in Guilford Co on waters of S Buffelow Cr; border: on W by his own land and on S & E by James Causbey & John Toms.

page 96
2731 (25). Mar. 14, 1793 John Brinchfield enters 6 ac in Guilford Co on waters of Haw R; border: James Warnock, on E of Betty Moore, & his own land.

2732 (26). Mar. 28, 1793 Michael Witt enters 40 ac in Guilford Co on waters of Redy fork; border: on E by his own land, on S & W by Martin Wyruk, & on N by Frederick Smith.

2733 (27). Mar. 28, 1793 Micael Witt enters 20 ac in Guilford Co on waters of Redy fork; border: on W & N by William Downey, Joseph Mast on E, & on S by Francis Swisher.

2734 (28). Mar. 29, 1793 Benjamin Morgan enters 100 ac in Guilford Co on waters of Stinking Quarter Cr; border: on E & W by Philip Shew, on N by George Limebury, & on S by James Oneal.

2735 (29). May 1, 1793 Philip Shew (or Shaw) enters 40 ac in Guilford Co on waters of Stinkin Quarter Cr; border: George Clap on S, George Shoffner on W, John Coble, & on E by Orange County line.

2736 (30). May 8, 1793 Fletcher Silivan (or Sulivant) enters 86 ac in Guilford Co on waters of Stinkin Quarter Cr; border: his own land on E, Thomas Low on S, & Solomon Grace on N.

2737 (31). May 20, 1793 Richard Day enters 70 ac in Guilford Co on waters of Deep R; border: on E by his own land, on N by Matthew Coffin, on W by James Gilleland, on S by Benjamin Merrel.

page 97
2738 (32). May 20, 1793 Nathan Gladson enters 7.5 ac in Guilford Co on waters of Redy fork; border: on E by John Walker and on W by William Lukus.

2739 (33). May 20, 1793 James Person enters 150 ac in Guilford Co on waters of Deep R; border: on E by Dinis Tomey, Randolph [County] line on S, & Dr(?) Caldwell on N.

2740 (34). caveated by Jacob Arment and John Lamb "each a part"; virdit in favor of cavitors warrants issued. May 20, 1793 Curtis Langerel enters 150 ac in Guilford Co on waters of Pole catt Cr; border: Salley Swim and John Leonard.

2741 (35). May 21, 1793 John Harvel (or Howel) enters 90 ac in Guilford Co on waters of Deep R; border: entry "he" purchased from Peter Dent.

2742 (36). Jun. 11, 1793 Nathaniel Simpson enters 30 ac in Guilford Co on waters of Redy fork; border: his own line, Samuel Maxwell, & Thomas Maxwell.

2743 (37). Aug. 9, 1793 Edward Millis enters 70 ac in Guilford Co on waters of S Buffalow Cr; border: Swain, Whealer, Stack, & his own land.

2744 (38). Aug. 20,1 793 Alexander Johnson enters 100 ac in Guilford Co on waters of Pole cat Cr; border: Thomas Johnson's N corner, William Dickey, old Aydlet, James Dickey, & William Swim.

page 98
2745 (39). Aug. 20, 1793 William Swim enters 100 ac in Guilford Co on waters of Pole cat Cr; border: his own land, James Dickey, Barna McCollum, Andrew Carmichal, & Joseph Meacy.

2746 (40). Aug. 20, 1793 John McClain enters 20 ac in Guilford Co on waters of Alemance Cr on both sides said creek; border: Jesse McComb on E and John Smith on N; part of old entry of said McClain (write over).

2747 (41). withdrawn; no warrant issued. Aug. 23, 1793 James Gilleland enters 50 ac in Guilford Co on waters of Rich fork of Abots Cr; border: his own land, Matthew Coffin, & Richard Day.

2748 (42). Sept. 2, 1793 William Shearer (or Sheaver) jr enters 40 ac in Guilford Co on S side of Great Allemance Cr; border: said William Sheaver on N and Adam Starr on W.

2749 (43). Sept. 7, 1793 James Porter enters 25 ac in Guilford Co on waters of Great Allimance Cr; border: on S by Capt. Albright, on W by Adam Soots, & on N by said Porter; "being of triangular figure".

2750 (44). Oct. 3, 1793 Thomas Low enters 190 ac on waters of Stinking Quarter Cr; border: on E by Hutton & Sulivan, on N by Graus, on W by Hunter, & on S by widow Low.

2751 (45). withdrawn & no warrant to issue "No" & money transfered to David Shearer. Oct. 14, 1793 [following entry lined out] John Jordan enters 50 ac on Rock Run of Allemance Cr; border: Joseph Rumley on S, John Forbush on W, & James Montgomery on N; "this entry crossed out in the original Book thus & the number caried on".

page 99
2752 (2nd 45). Oct. 15, 1793 David Shearer enters 100 ac in Guilford Co on Rock Run of Allemance Cr; border: a late survey of Joseph Rumley on S, John & Betty Forbush on W, & James Montgomery desc on N.

2753 (46). Nov. 19, 1793 Dennis Toomey enters 48 ac on W side of his "plantation" where he lives on head of Waltons Br; border: William Montgomery and Doctor Caldwell.

2754 (47). Nov. 19, 1793 caveated by Nathan Hunt "so far as" 23 ac; caveat "comprimised" & warrant issued agreeable to order of court. Nov. 19, 1793 Thomas Archer enters 30 ac in Guilford Co on waters of (blank); border: his own SE corner, George Hodgin, Nathan Hunt, & Evan Stephens.

2755 (48). Dec. 5, 1793 John Johnson enters 86 ac in Guilford Co on waters of Pole cat Cr; border: Andrew Carminal, William Hickman, William Fields, & Hugh Sherwood.

2756 (49). Jan. 23, 1794 James Sarratt enters 100 ac in Guilford Co on waters of Porters Cr a branch of Redy fork; border: on N by Shaw, on W by his own land, & on S by James Flack.

2757 (50). Jan. 24, 1794 Jacob Swisher jr enters 17 ac in Guilford Co on waters of Redy fork; border: Michael Witt, Joseph Mast, John Swisher, & Francis Swisher.

2758 (51). Jan. 25, 1794 Thomas Gault enters 30 ac in Guilford Co on waters of N Buffelow Cr; border: Watson Wharton on E, William Ranken on S, James Donnel on W, & his own land on N.

page 100
2759 (52). Jan. 25, 1794 Thomas Gault enters 10 ac on waters of Redy fork; border: on E by Mical Witt, on S by his own land, & on N by William Downey.

2760 (53). Feb. 15, 1794 Catherine McCalep (or McCaleb), relect of John McCalep desc, in behalf of Jean McCalep, enters 80 ac on Redy fork of Haw R; border: on E by Orange [County] line, on S by Luke Pendergrass, & on W by Nichlas Gift; includes "the" improvement.

2761 (54). Feb. 18, 1794 William Armfield III enters 70 ac in Guilford Co on waters of N Buffalow Cr; border: William Armfield on W, on N by William Armfield II, his own land on E, & John Armfield on S.

2762 (55). Feb. 18, 1794 David Hoggatt enters 84 ac in Guilford Co in fork of Deep R; border: Joel Sanders on NW corner.

2763 (56). Feb. 21, 1794 James Shelley enters 50 ac in on waters of Deep R; border: John Standfield's NE corner, said Shelley's line, & Hyatt.

2764 (57). Mar. 1, 1794 Reuben Bunker enters 280 ac in Guilford Co on Bull Run waters of Deep R; border: on W by William Gardner & Mesheek Couch on W, Henry Camplin, Leven Williams, & Timothy Macy; includes his improvement.

2765 (58). Mar. 11, 1794 Nichles Coble enters 100 ac in Guilford Co on waters of Stinking Quarter Cr; border: said Nichles Coble, widow Carrick, Henry Grace, Thomas Bugum, & Samuel Wanter.

2766 (59). Apr. 6, 1794 Robert Thompson enters 130 ac in Guilford Co on Redy fork waters; border: deeded land of John Cunningham and Robert Thompson desc.

page 101
2767 (60). Apar. 24, 1794 Levi Weatherly enters 30 ac in Guilford Co on waters of Allemance Cr; border: William Weatherly on E, Thomas Woodburn on N, Jobe Weatherley on W, & Peter Kirkman on S.

2768 (61). Apr. 26, 1794 Peter Wagoner enters 40 ac in Guilford Co on waters of Rock Cr; border: John Wagoner, Suton, & Peter Wagoner's own land.

2769 (62). May 17, 1794 Philip Burrow jr enters 50 ac in Guilford Co on waters of Stinking Quarter Cr; border: Philip Burrow sr on S, Lodiwick Clap on W, on N by Dent & Greeson (or Gruson), & on E by Low.

2770 (63). May 19, 1794 Fletcher Sulivan enters 60 ac in Guilford Co on waters of Stinking Quarter Cr; border: his own survey and Lodwick Clap.

2771 (64). May 19, 1794 Roger Layton enters 100 ac in Guilford Co on waters of Stinking Quarter Cr; border: Solomon Grace, Thaddeus Bell, & Elias Cowan.

2772 (65). May 20, 1794 Lodiwick Clap, son of John Philip Clap, enters 60 ac in Guilford Co on waters of Stinking Quarter Cr; border: his own land, a late entry of Philip Burrow, & Thaddeus Bell.

2773 (66). May 20, 1794 Nathan Hunt enters 33.5 ac on Long Br of Deep R; border: his own NE corner and Thomas Archer.

page 102

2774 (67). May 21, 1794 Joseph Leonard enters 300 ac in Guilford Co on waters of Pole cat Cr; border: deeded land of John Leonard on N, on W by John Stone, Joseph Worth on S, & John Lamb on E.

2775 (68). May 23, 1794 Thomas Johnson enters 16 ac in Guilford Co on waters of Pole cat Cr; border: his own S corner, Swim, & John Johnson.

2776 (69). Jun. 7, 1794 Quintin Nicks jr enters 50 ac in Guilford Co on waters of N Buffelow Cr; border: John Nicks corner, John Gillaspie, Thos Black, Gaster, & Capt. Rankin.

2777 (70) Aug. 1, 1794 Curtis Langcrell enters 75 ac in Guilford Co on Stinking Quarter Cr; border: Thomas Low, widow Low, Samuel Hunter, George Hutton, & Nickles Coble.

2778 (71). Aug. 27, 1794 Joseph Gullett enters 90 ac in Guilford Co on waters of S Buffalow and Allemance Creeks; border: on E by his own [land] & Thomas Dawson and on W by Gorrel Kerr & Donnell; within limits of old survey purchased by said Gullett & Dawson from Francis McBride.

2779 (72). Sept. 18, 1794 Richard Linsichum enters 70 ac in Guilford Co on waters of Pole cat Cr; border: Sarah Mash, Hodson, Allen Wilson, & Reynolds.

page 103

2780 (73). withdrawn; no warrant issued. Oct 3, 1794 William Quiet (or Quait) sr enters 40 ac in Guilford Co on branch of Little Allemance Cr; border: on E & S side of his own land; within limits of his own old survey.

2781 (74). Nov. 10, 1794 Philip Burrow enters 50 ac in Guilford Co on waters of Stinking Quarter Cr; border: Ginkin Sulivant and William Dent.

2782 (75). Dec. 16, 1794 James Oneal enters 100 ac in Guilford Co on waters of Stinking Quarter Cr; border: on W by Jenkin Sulivant and the "other two squares" by his own land.

2783 (76). Dec. 16, 1794 Samuel Frazer enters 28 ac in Guilford Co on S fork of Buffelow Cr; border: his own corner.

2784 (77). Jan. 3, 1795 Henry Davis enters 60 ac in Guilford Co on waters of Deep R; border: Bowman, William Raper's homsteed, James Calwell, & N side of said Raper's new survey.

2785 (78). Jan. 17, 1795 Fletcher Sulivan enters 54 ac in Guilford Co on waters of Stinking Quarter Cr; border: his own late survey, Bell, & Clap.
2786 (79). Jan. 17, 1795 Roger Layton enters 80 ac in Guilford Co on waters of Stinkin Quarter Cr; border: his own late survey, Elias Cowen, & Thomas Bingham.

2787 (80). caveated by Ephraim Hermon "20"; John Ellet withdraws this entry; money returned; no warrant to issue. Jan. 17, 1795 John Ellet enters 100 ac in Guilford Co on waters of Stinking Quarter Cr; border: widow Low's S corner, Barney McColm, & George Hutton.

page 104
2788 (81). Jan. 17, 1795 Nathaniel Grace enters 100 ac in Guilford Co on waters of Stinking Quarter Cr; border: his own corner and Randolph [County] line.

2789 (82). Jan. 17, 1795 William Green enters 75 ac in Guilford Co on waters of Stinking Quarter Cr; border: Henry Green, Soloman Grace, & Nathaniel Grace.

2790 (83). Jan. 20, 1795 Ephraim Hermon enters 150 ac in Guilford Co on waters of Stinking Quarter Cr; border: widow Low, Hunter, & Randolph [County] line; includes his improvement.

page 105
Guilford Co, NC letter certifys this book contains complete transcript of books kept by entry takers in Guilford Co between Dec. 1777 and Feb. 8, 1795; book kept by Ralph Gorrel esq "he says was taken by British Army when at his house in 1781"; transcript was examined by "select" committee.
Bonds: (1) bond in "my office" signed by Ralph Gorrel with William Cusick, John White, & George Cortner as securities to Richard Caswell esq, governor, for 8,000£ for performance of duties of entry taker dated Feb. 17, 1770 that he was appointed entry taker for Guilford Co; (2) bond in "my office" signed by William Dent with Ja Martin, Jas Hunter, & Henry Whitsel as securities to Richard Caswell esq, governor, for 8,000£ for performance of duties as entry taker dated Nov. 16, 1779 that he was entry taker for Guilford Co; no other records of either of their appointments in "my office" greater part of which was destroyed by British Army in 1781 "Mar. 18".
At Aug. court 1783 William Dent esq was "continued" entry taker for Guilford Co giving bound and security of 10,000£ a piece; at Nov. court 1787 on regisnation of William Dent esq Alexander McKeen esq was appointed entry taker by court and he gave bond for 2,000£ with Hance Hamilton and John Hamilton securities; at Feb. court 1792 on regsnation of Alexander McKeen esq, John Sarratt esq was appointed entry taker for Guilford Co and had bond of 2,000£ with John Hamilton security payable to Alexr Martin esq, governor.
Signed Jul. 21, 1796 in 21st year of our Independence. John Hamilton cc.

Following entrys (2791-2969) taken from "Secretary of State entry takers' returns Gar-Gui 1759-1904 (SS 561) Guilford Co (1787-1900) folder". This folder contains many loose sheets listing entrys for a specific time period. Usually less information is given about the entrys than found in the preceeding entry book. The entrys abstracted here cover the period 1787-Dec. 1798. The folder also contains entry summarys for periods from Oct. 1800 to Mar. 1900. The entry number were assigned to continue the number from the above entry book.

sheet 1 (no date)
2791 (1). Alexander Nelson enters 500 ac on both sides of Brush Cr in Guilford Co; border: John Clark, Henry Mitchel, & Peter King; surveyed & "returned to Secretary's office" for him as part of tract that Joshua Edwards, a Quaker, purchased some years ago before "commencement of the present War" and he has resided there ever since; "I" believe it was an entry in the former land office.

2792 (2). William White enters 94 ac on Brush Cr in Guilford Co; border: Aaron Mendenhall and John Clark; surveyed & returned to Secretary's office & is near Jacob Hunt a Quaker's improvement; where he resides.

2793 (3). Maj. John Nelson enters 360 ac on both sides of Moons Cr in Guilford Co; border: William Robinson; surveyed & returned to Secretary's office; includes part of Jacob Hunt's improvement and all improvements of Abner Hunt, Isham Hunt, & William Hunt; part of entry was formerly surveyed "(as I am well informed)" for Doctor John Park and by him & Hugh Forster sold to Jonathan & John Unthanks for "valuable" consideration & by John Unthank (since the said Jonathan's desc) sold or given to aforesaid Abner, Isham, & William Hunts who are all of the Society of people called Quakers.

sheet 2 "following is a list of entries made as entry taker of Guilford Co during "my appointment" to said office [Alex McKeen]; oath at end of list Oct. 3, 1789 Alex McKee esq, entry taker, for Guilford Co to J Hamilton JP.
[on back of page:] #172 Alexr McKeen entry taker Guilford £435.15.
2794 (1). Dec. 24, 1787 Owen Lane enters 40 ac   £4.
2795 (2). Dec. 24, 1787 Hance Hamilton esq enters 50 ac   £5.
2796 (3). Feb. 7, 1788 Daniel Shurwood enters 80 ac   £8.
2797 (4). Feb. 18, 1788 John Hall enters 100 ac   £10.
2798 (5). Mar. 29, 1788 John McAdow enters 50 ac   £5.
2799 (6). Mar. 29, 1788 John McBride enters 50 ac   £5.
2800 (7). May 2, 1788 Adam Mitchel enters 200 ac   £20.
2801 (8). May 19, 1788 Joseph Truet enters 10 ac   £10.
2802 (9). May 20, 1788 David Hodson enters 107 ac   £10.14.
2803 (10). Jun. 11, 1788 James Warnoch enters 50 ac   £5.

2804 (11). Aug. 16, 1788 Benjamin Merrel enters 170 ac   £17.

2805 (12). Aug. 21, 1788 Ralph Garrel esq enters 40 ac   £4.

2806 (13). Aug. 21, 1788 James McAdow enters 37 ac   £3.14.

2807 (14). Aug. 22, 1788 Elizabeth Scott enters 80 ac   £8.

2808 (15). Sept. 23, 1788 James Thompson enters 120 ac   £12.

2809 (16). Oct. 1, 1788 George Crisman enters 20 ac   £2.

2810 (17). Oct. 1, 1788 Christian Tall enters 160 ac   £16.

2811 (18). Oct. 8, 1788 John Stephenson enters 40 ac   £4.

2812 (19). Oct. 10, 1788 Abner Weatherley enters 60 ac   £6.

2813 (20). Oct. 14, 1788 Daniel McMin enters 150 ac   £15.

2814 (21). Nov. 19, 1788 John Ocia enters 50 ac   £5.

2815 (22). Nov. 19, 1788 Daniel May enters 150 ac   £15.

2816 (23). Dec. 5, 1788 Wiliam Hilton enters 100 ac   £10.

2817 (24). Dec. 8, 1788 Mardicah Mendinghall enters 412 ac   £41.4.

2818 (25). Dec. 9, 1788 Valintine Mileham enters 120 ac   £12.

2819 (26). Dec. 26, 1788 John Haley and John Hamilton enter 300 ac   £30.

2820 (27). Dec. 26, 1788 Martha Tasey enters 200 ac   £20.

2821 (28). Dec. 27, 1788 Thomas Archer enters 30 ac   £3.

2822 (29). Dec. 27, 1788 "the same" enters 20 ac   £2.

2823 (30). Jan. 8, 1789 John Gilcrest enters 300 ac   £30.

2824 (31). Jan. 10, 1789 Laven Williams enters 250 ac   £25.

2825 (32). Jan. 13, 1789 Thomas Crouch enters 50 ac   £5.

2826 (33). Jan. 19, 1789 George Heckman enters 9.5 ac   £0.19.

2827 (34). Jan. 24, 1789 Jonathan Hodson enters 76 ac   £7.12.

2828 (35). Jan. 27, 1789 Hartwell Barham enters 74 ac   £7.8.

2829 (36). Jan. 28, 1789 Robert Thompson enters 100 ac   £10.

2830 (37). Feb. 6, 1789 Peter Rian Simpson enters 122 ac   £12.4.

2831 (38). Feb. 13, 1789 Hance & John Hamilton and J H Spruce enter 50 ac £5.

2832 (39). Feb. 16, 1789 William Dickey enters 90 ac   £9.

2833 (40). Feb. 25, 1789 Charles Bruce esq enters 12 ac   £1.4.

2834 (41). Apr. 6, 1789 John Farbush enters 125 ac   £12.10.

2835 (42). May 8, 1789 William Montgomery enters 45 ac   £4.10.

2836 (43). May 25, 1789 John Wolfington enters 150 ac   £15.

sheet 3 Alexander McKeen, entry taker in Guilford Co, for land entered May 25 to Dec. 31, 1789.

2837 (1). Jun. 6, 1789 Simon Moon enters 112 ac   £11.4.

2838 (2). Jul. 14, 1789 Henery Whitrel enters 60 ac   £6.

2839 (3). Aug. 12, 1789 Christian Fall enters 350 ac   £35.

2840 (4). Aug. 18, 1789 William Wait enters 50 ac   £5.

2841 (5). Aug. 23, 1789 Thomas Harpen enters 212.5 ac   £21.5.

2842 (6). Sept. 4, 1789 Joseph Standley enters 60 ac   £6.

2843 (7). Dec. 1, 1789 John Gillaspie enters 150 ac   £15.

2844 (8). Dec. 14, 1789 Abigail Wilson enters 200 ac   £20.

2845 (9). Dec. 27, 1789 George Hamilton enters 60 ac   £6.
2846 (10). Dec. 28, 1789 Stephen Sinnen enters 60 ac   £6.
above entrys certified Aug. 2, 1790 by Alexdr McKeen, Et.

sheet 4 Land entrys for Guilford Co from Jan. 1, 1793 to Dec. 31, 1793 (a printed form).
2847 (20). Jan. 21 Christian Fall enters 6 ac.
2848 (21). Feb. 15 Mathew Coffin enters 150 ac.
2849 (22). Feb. 15 Patrick McGibbony enters 50 ac.
2850 (23). Feb. 22 George Wyatt enters 40 ac.
2851 (24). Feb. 24 John Hubbard enters 50 ac.
2852 (25). Mar. 14 John Brenchfield enters 6 ac.
2853 (26). Mar. 28 Micael Witt enters 40 ac.
2854 (27). Mar. 28 Micaell Witt enters 20 ac.
2855 (28). Mar. 29 Ben Morgan enters 100 ac.
2856 (29). May 1 Phillip Shews enters 40 ac.
2857 (30). May 8 Fletcher Sulivan enters 86 ac.
2858 (31). May 20 Richard Day enters 70 ac.
2859 (32). May 20 Nathan Gladson enters 7 ac.
2860 (33). May 20 James Parrsons enters 150 ac.
2861 (34). May 20 caveated and lost.
2862 (35). May 21 John Howell enters 90 ac.
2863 (36). Jun. 11 Nathan Simpson enters 30 ac.
2864 (37). Aug. 9 Edward Millis enters 70 ac.
2865 (38). Aug. 20 Allexander Johnson enters 100 ac.
2866 (39). Aug. 20 William Sweim enters 100 ac.
2867 (40). Aug. 20 John McClain enters 20 ac.
2868 (41). Sept. 2 withdrawn
2869 (42). Sept. 2 William Sheaver enters 40 ac.
2870 (43). Sept. 7 James Porter enters 25 ac.
2871 (44). Oct. 3 Thomas Low enters 190 ac.
2872 (45). Oct. 14 David Shearer enters 100 ac.
2873 (46). Nov. 19 Thomas Archer enters 30 ac.
2874 (47). Nov. 19 Dennis Toomy enters 48 ac.
2875 (48). Dec. 5 John Johnson enters 86 ac.
above certified May 24, 1794 by John Starrat esq, entry taker, to George Finley, JP.   Written on back of sheet: "it is to be remembered that numbers 46 & 47 were misplaced in taking of the book."

sheet 5 List of entrys for Guilford Co from Jan. 1 to Mar. 20, 1795 "after which time the entry taker left off to receive anymore than his own fee."
2876 (77). Jan. 3 Henry Davis enters 60 ac.
2877 (78). Jan. 17 Fletcher Suilvan enters 54 ac.
2878 (79). Jan. 17 Roger Layton enters 80 ac.

2879 (80). was caveated and withdrawn; entered by "cavitor" at No. 83 [see more after #2891].

2880 (81). Jan. 17 Nathaniel Grace enters 100 ac.

2881 (82). Jan. 17 William Greens enters 75 ac.

2882 (83). Jan. 20 Ephraim Hermon enters 150 ac [see more after #2891].

2883 (84). Feb. _?_ William Quiet (write over) enters 54 ac [see more after #2891].

2884 (85). Feb. 11 George McKnny enters 50 ac.

2885 (86). Feb. 11 Nathaniel Peoples enters 40 ac.

2886 (87). Feb. 17 John Coe enters 10 ac.

2887 (88). Feb. 18 Jesse Dillan enters 25 ac.

2888 (89). for money already paid __?__ serry (write over) [see more after #2891].

2889 (90). Mar. 10 John Swing enters 60 ac.

2890 (91). Mar. 18 Jacob Coeble enters 50 ac.

2891 (92). Mar. 20 Edward Peargram enters 50 ac.

certified Oct. 29, 1795 by John Starrat esq, entry taker, to George Wilson, JP. John Starrat didn't "new acts" had taken place until after Mar. 20 when he got the account thereof in the public papers.   Following written on back of sheet: "Law requires whole of entrys made with you from Jan. 1 to time you knew the law was altered; therefore you must collect money for #84 & 89 and return number of acres entered & also explain whether #80 was taken by #83 that is whether same land is entered by Ephraim Hermon--(signed) JC.   #89 has been paid for by the person entering under act of 1795 as per receipt #253 (or 283) __?__ book--(signed) JC.   Land entered by Ephraim Harmon #83 withdrawn by one Elliot #80; Harmon cavittes him under entry made in Randolph [County] in which county he supposed the land on which he lived lay; Elliott withdrew(?) his entry & Harmon then entered the land in Guilford [Co]--(signed) John Starrat Oct. 4, 1790(?)."

sheet 6 List of entrys from Mar. 20 to Dec. 31, 1795.

2892 (93). Apr. 22 David Gillim enters 39 ac; no warrant issued.

2893 (94). Apr. 25 William Gamble and Jeremiah Forbies enter 50 ac; warrant issued.

2894 (95). May 13 Andrew Willson enters 20 ac; warrant issued.

2895 (96). May 15 George Forbies enters 150 ac; warrant issued.

2896 (97). May 15 John Lane enters 60 ac; no warrant issued.

2897 (98). May 19 William Hitchcock enters 40 ac; warrant issued.

2898 (99). May 22 Jacob Arment enters 150 ac; warrant issued.

2899   [following lined out:] May 22 Adam Starr enters 60 ac dropt his claim.

2900 (100). May 22 Mordecai Lane enters 100 ac; wart. issued.

2901 (101). May 22 Adam Starr enters 60 ac; dropt his claim.

2902 (102). Jun. 27 Curtis Langrell enters 300 ac; warrant issued.

2903 (103). Aug. 3 Hezekiah Wheeler enters 42 ac; warrant issued.

2904 (104). Aug. 20 George Trotter enters 40 ac; warrant issued.
2905 (105). Sept. 7 William and David Mayben enters 220 ac; warrant issued.
2906 (106). Oct. 30 John Lamb enters 220 ac; warrant issued.
2907 (107). Nov. 16 William Bridges enters 90 ac; warrant issued.
2908 (108). Nov. 23 Sipple Harvey enters 40 ac; warrant issued.
2909 (109). Nov. 28 Jacob Shearer enters 30 ac; warrant issued.
2910 (110). Dec. 29 Jacob Kenut enters 18 ac; warrant issued.
2911 (111). Dec. 30 Andrew Carmichal enters 50 ac; warrant issued.
certified Nov. 14, 1798 by John Starrat, entry taker, to H McCain.
sheet 7 List of entrys from Jan. 1, 1796 to Dec. 31, 1796.
2912 (112). Jan. 9 Thomas and William Nelson enter 120 ac; warrant issued.
2913 (113). Jan. 12 Andrew Flack enters 40 ac; warrant issued.
2914 (114). Jan. 26 Aaron Creenor enters 110 ac; warrant issued.
2915 (115). Jan. 26 James Leister enters 100 ac; warrant issued.
2916 (116). Jan. 26 Aaron Creanor enters 30 ac; warrant issued.
2917 (117). Feb. 3 Nimrod Jester enters 50 ac; warrant issued.
2918 (118). Feb. 16 Hance McKain enters 18 ac; warrant issued.
2919 (119). Feb. 27 James Daning, for John North, enters 100 ac; warrant issued.
2920 (120). Mar. 24 Jesse McComb enters 48.25 ac; warrant issued.
2921 (121). May 6 George Nicks enters 68 ac; warrant issued.
2922 (122). May 18 George Nicks enters 50 ac; (blank).
2923 (123). May 29 John Brenchfield enters 89 ac; warrant issued.
2924 (124). Aug. 12 Andrew Finley enters 25 ac; warrant issued.
2925 (125). Sept. 3 Daniel Gillaspie enters 284 ac; warrant issued.
2926 (126). Sept. 19 Abraham Chrisman enters 75 ac; warrant issued.
2927 (127). Nov. 22 David Karr enters 15 ac; warrant issued.
2928 (128). Nov. 22 Richard Orsment enters 100 ac; warrant issued.
2929 (129). Nov. 22 John Frazer enters 20 ac; warrant issued.
2930 (130). Nov. 22 William Lane and Jonathan Parker enter 150 ac; warrant isssued.
2931 (131). Nov. 22 William Armfield enters 100 acc; warrant issued.
2932 (132). Nov. 22 Joel Hyat enters 36 ac; warrant issued.
2933 (133). Nov. 23 Ann Boyd enters 50 ac; warrant issued.
2934 (134). Dec. 1 Ephraim Frotter enters 80 ac; warrant issued.
2935 (135). Dec. 15 John Cooper enters 150 ac; warrant issued.
2936 (136). Dec. 23 Jesse Field enters 35 ac; warrant issued.
certified Nov. 14, 1798 by John Starrat to H McCain.

sheet 8 List of entrys from Jan. 1, 1798 to Dec. 31, 1798.
2937 (179). Jan. 10 Isaac Widow jr enters 15 ac.
2938 (180). Jan. 10 Isaa Widows sr enters 25 ac.
2939 (181). Jan. 15 John Adgen enters 100 ac.
2940 (182). Jan. 20 David Caldwell DD enters 150 ac.

2941 (183). Feb. 15 Andrew Donnel enters 18 ac.
2942 (184). Feb. 20 Andrew Gibson enters 150 ac.
2943 (185). Mar. 5 John Vanstorie enters 39 ac.
2944 (186). Mar. 5 John Vanstorie enters 50 ac.
2945 (187). Mar. 31 Levi Coffin enters 60 ac.
2946 (188). Apr. 16 James Walker enters 40 ac.
2947 (189). Apr. 26 Ashur Hyatt enters 16 ac.
2948 (190). Apr. 26 Howel Parker enters 13 ac; no warrant.
2949 (191). May 1 William Dillon enters 50 ac.
2950 (192). May 5 Alexander Gray jr enters 60 ac.
2951 (193). May 16 John Hunt enters 26 ac.
2952 (194). May 21 Georg Haworth enters 22 ac.
2953 (195). May 25 James Camplin enters 60 ac.
2954 (196). May 25 Jesse Dillon enters 20 ac.
2955 (197). Jun. 16 John Vanstorie enters 75 ac.
2956 (198). Jun. 16 John Vanstorie enters 45 ac.
2957 (199). Jun. 16 John Vanstorie enters 22 ac.
2958 (200). Jun. 16 John Vanstorie enters 35 ac.
2959 (201). Jun. 18 David Brown enters 10 ac.
2960 (202). Jun. 18 John Vanstorie enters 30 ac.
2961 (203). Jul. 19 Andrew Wilson enters 60 ac.
2962 (204). Aug. 21 Cornelus Cook enters 100 ac.
2963 (205). Aug. 21 Hery Cook enters 300 ac.
2964 (206). Aug. 21 John Standley enters 100 ac.
2965 (207). Sept. 8 John Hitchcock enters 60 ac.
2966 (208). Sept. 8 Isaac Frazer enters 20 ac.
2967 (209). Nov. 6 Charles Sillivan enters 40 ac.
2968 (210). Nov. 7 Adam Sutz enters 20 ac.
2969 (211). Dec. 24 James Smith enters 60 ac.
certified May 20, 1799 by John Sarrat esq, entry taker, to H McCain.

Rockingham Co Land Entry 1790-1795 SS 964.1 (book 2) and 964.2 (book 3); one entry per page.

Book 2
R89. Dec. 29, 1790 William Clark jr enters 50 ac in Rockingham Co; border: John Matlock, Thomas Allen, & Josiah Little.

R90. Dec. 29, 1790 James Hodge enters 200 ac in Rockingham Co on waters of Hogans Cr; border: John Hodge desc, Samuel Watt, Joseph Payne, & Joshua Wright.

R91. Jan. 5, 1791 Elijah Brown enters 58 ac in Rockingham Co on waters of Hogans Cr; border: Elijah Brown's corner of a former entry "in the county line", Samuel Watt, & James Gills.

R92. Jan. 29, 1791 Guy Oermilion enters 13 ac in Rockingham Co; border: John Mackey, John McCarrie, & claimant's own land.

R93. Feb. 7, 1791 Nathaniel Linder enters 100 ac in Rockingham Co on waters of Jacobs Cr and on S of his own land; border: Joseph Cunningham.

R94. Feb. 22, 1791 James Hopewell enters 200 ac in Rockingham Co on waters of Wolf Island Cr; border: Jumping Br, another branch that runs into said creek, & joins John Linders.

R95. Mar. 9, 1791 Andrew Martin sr entrs 146 ac in Rockingham Co on Rocky fork of Troublesom Cr; border: his former survey.

R96. Apr. 16, 1791 Alexander Martin esq enters 50 ac in Rockingham Co; border: his "Qarter" on main branch of Jacobs Cr called Rolston's plantation; at or near SE corner of same.

R97. Apr. 29, 1791 William Bethell esq enters 200 ac in Rockingham Co on waters of Wolf Island Cr on N side thereof; border: William Self's corner and Mr Marr's line.

R98. Jun. 13, 1791 Robert Small enters 100 ac in Rockingham Co on Glady Br of Big Troublesom Cr; border: claimant's own line, across said branch, & "round" to William Miller.

R99. Aug. 20, 1791 Stokes Yoeman enters 100 ac in Rockingham Co on Dan R; border: George Peay, John May, & bent(?) tract where Drury Yoeman lives.

R100. Aug. 22, 1791 Henry Scales enters 50 ac in Rockingham Co; border: his own land.

R101. Aug. 27, 1791 John Olliver enters 50 ac in Rockingham Co on both sides of Hogans Cr; border: Robert Gilleland on W and his own land on N.

R102. Sept. 10, 1791 John Caldwell enters 100 ac in Rockingham Co on waters of Dan R; border: Alexander McClaran, William Aston, & claimant's own line.

R103. Occt. 1, 1791 Henry Pratt enters 100 ac in Rockingham Co on waters of Jacobs Cr; border: near Oldham Short's corner tree.

R104. Oct. 8, 1791 Robert Cumming enters 100 ac in Rockingham Co on waters of Haw R; border: Jonas Frost and John Blackburn.

R105. Nov. 29, 1791 Mathew Peggs enters 50 ac in Rockingham Co; border: William Callums and William Mills corner on the Green Spring, and between Callums, Mills, & Richard Cardwell.

R106. entry was drawn Dec. 23, 1791. Nov. 29, 1791 Hezekiah Carry enters 103 ac in Rockingham Co on waters of Big Troublesom Cr on head of Kings Br; border: Charles Bruce, former survey "my" own, John Bowen, & Ephraim Thompson.

R107. Dec. 23, 1791 Hezekiah Carry enters 203 ac in Rockingham Co on waters of Big Troublesom Cr on head of Kings Br; border: Charles Bruce, former survey "my" own, & John Bowen.

R108. Dec. 24, 1791 Michael Caffey enters 100 ac in Rockingham Co on S side of Big Troublesom Cr; border or near: Hugh Linches or William Buchanans.

R109. Feb. 24, 1791(sic) Nathaniel Linder enters 64 ac in Rockingham Co; border: his own deeded land, Cunningham, & Ezekiel Wright.

one blank page.

R110. Aug. 31, 1792 Robert Joyce enters 80 ac in Rockingham Co on waters of Fishers Cr; border: Philip Deathredge desc and claimant's own line.

R111. Sept. 4, 1792 James Roach enters 50 ac on waters of Bigg Rockhouse Cr in Rockingham Co; border: Theophelous Spurrier and Luke Bernard.

R112. Sept. 15, 1792 Elmore Walker sr enters 80 ac in Rockingham Co on waters of Mosses Cr; border: Thomas Henderson, widow Scury, & "my" own [land].

R113. Sept. 20, 1792 Shadrak Lewis enters 100 ac in Rockingham Co on waters of Mosses Cr; border: Thomas Henderson and "my" own line.

R114. Sept. 25, 1792 James Hayes sr enters 100 ac on N side of waters of Brushey fork of Jacobs Cr; border: his own land "on upper tract", "the Governors", Pleasant Henderson, & John Carners.

R115. Sept. 26, 1791 Joseph McCulloch enters 73 ac on head waters of Hogans Cr; border: Hodges, Joseph Payns crossroad survey, & claimant's own land.

R116. Oct. 11, 1792 Aaron Allin enters 15 ac on waters of Brushey fork of Bigg Rockhouse Cr in Rockingham Co; border: South side William Jones latest entry.

R117. Oct. 11, 1792 Alexander McClaran and Abraham Philips esq enter 100 ac on waters of Big Rockhouse Cr; border: Jesse Walker and Corry Fitts.

R118. Oct. 22, 1792 William Flemming enters 300 ac; border: his own land on E, Charles Bruce, & John Chadwell; includes forks of Bruce's and Baggage road.

R119. Oct. 22, 1792 Thomas Henderson esq enters 200 ac; border: late entry made in William Clark's office on S side, Charles Bruce on E, & John Chadwell on W.

R120. Oct. 27, 1792 Thomas Rafferty enters 200 ac in Rockingham Co on waters of Town Cr; border: Allumby Williams, widow Browder, & "my" own lines.

R121. Nov. 27, 1792 William Callahan enters 50 ac; border: Virginia line on white oak branded "W".

R122. Nov. 29, 1792 John Scorden enters 100 ac in Rockingham Co on waters of Clouds Cr; border: William Proctor.

R123. Dec. 22, 1792 David Alexander enters 100 ac in Rockingham Co; border: Henry Seales, Minerd Collsy (or Collay), & John Hill.

R124. Dec. 22, 1792 Robert Larimer enters 200 ac in Rockingham Co on waters of Curbys Cr; border: widow Lacy, Governor Martin, & Francis Four.

R125. Jan. 3, 1793 John Richey enters 99 ac in Rockingham Co; border: Adam Tate, William Grady, John Brown, & Thomas Carter.

R126. Jan. 3, 1793 David Lovel enters 81 ac on Piney fork of Town Cr; border: William Dennis, Cornelius Mabrey, & Joseph Porter.

R127. entry withdrawn Apr. 2, 1793. Jan. 4, 1793 Hugh Linch enters 100 ac in Rockingham Co on S side of Big Troublesom Cr; border: running S from his own line.

R128. Jan. 5, 1793 Robert Lellie enters 50 ac in Rockingham Co on waters of Town Cr; border: "my" own line.

R129. Jan. 17, 1793 Robert Boak enters 40 ac on waters of Big Troublesom Cr in Rockingham Co; border: Mr. Hugh Linch.

R130. Jan. 22, 1793 George Russel enters 41 ac in Rockingham Co on waters of Mayo R; border: Andrew Hunter.

R131 Jan. 22, 1793 Peter Hunter enters 58 ac in Rockingham Co on waters of Mayo R; border: "my" own line.

R132 Jan. 22, 1793 Zachariah King enters 50 ac in Rockingham Co on waters of Mayo R; border: Champain Gibson.

R133. Jan. 22, 1793 Joseph Cunningham enters 50 ac in Rockingham Co on waters of Jacobs Cr; border: on W of "my" original line.

R134. Jan. 23, 1793 Abraham Philips esq enters 150 ac in Rockingham Co on waters of upper Hogans Cr and both sides of road leading by Fleming's; border or near: Charles Bruce and Moses Barrow; includes Tatom's preaching place.

R135. Jan. 23, 1793 John Strong enters 60 ac in Rockingham Co on waters of Buffellow Island Cr "adjoining and John Mines".

R136. number omitted; not in book.

R137. "mistake in number" entry withdrawn Mar. 9, 1793. Jan. 24, 1793 Andrew Robertson and Alexander McClaran enter 200 ac in Rockingham Co on waters of Town Cr; border: Allumby Williams and Rev. David Caldwell.

R138. entry withdrawn Mar. 9, 1793. Jan. 24, 1793 Alexander McClaran and Andrew Robertson enter 200 ac in Rockingham Co on waters of Fishers Cr; border: William Proctor and Charles Gallaway.

R139. Jan. 28, 1793 David Barnet enters 50 ac in Rockingham Co on waters of Still house Br; border: on N of Thomas Henderson.

R140. Feb. 1, 1793 John Jones enters 200 ac in Rockingham Co on both sides of Persimmon Br of Little Rockhouse Cr; border: a former survey of said Jones on E.

R141. Feb. 4,1 793 Nathaniel Linder enters 150 ac on waters of Jacobs Cr; border: Robert Martin and Thomas Lowe.

R142. entry withdrawn Apr. 13, 1793. Feb. 4, 1793 Nathaniel Linder enters 100 ac on waters of Jacobs Cr; border: Jacob Whitworth and John Deavers desc.

R143. entry withdrawn May 2, 1793. Feb. 7, 1793 William Bethell esq enters 300 ac in Rockingham Co on waters of Quacquaw Cr on both sides of said creek; border: Stephen Odear; includes place called the meadows.

R144. entry withdrawn May 2, 1793. Feb. 7, 1793 William Bethell esq enters 300 ac in Rockingham Co on both sides of Lick fork of Hogans Cr; between Thomas Chambers and William Barksdill.

R145. entry withdrawn Jun. 10, 1793. Feb. 12, 1793 Robert Small enters 200 ac in Rockingham Co on waters of Jacobs Cr; border: John Simmings and land known as Jones' old place.

R146. Feb. 12, 1793 Robert Small enters 100 ac in Rockingham Co; border: "beginning tree" of David Moore's the place "he" lives on, W to William Miller, and S to "his" own land.

R147. Feb. 14, 1793 Henry Seales enters 200 ac in Rockingham Co on waters of White Oak fork of Buffalo Island Cr; border: St. John Shropshiar.

R148. Feb. 16, 1793 Daniel Adkins enters 500 ac on waters of Lick fork of Wolf Island Cr; border: James Wardlaw, Samuel Herren, & John Hains.

R149. Feb. 18, 1793 Nathaniel Linder enters 200 ac on waters of Jacobs Cr and waters of Great Rockhouse Cr; border: "my" own [land].

R150. Feb. 18, 1793 Nathaniel Linder enters 150 ac on waters of Jacobs Cr; border: Martin Scury and "my" former entry.

R151. Feb. 27, 1793 John Burnes enters 98 ac in Rockingham Co on waters of Upper Hogans Cr; border: Thomas Henderson, Charles Bruce, & claimant's own land.

R152. (entry withdrawn May 13, 1793--erased). Feb. 28, 1793 John Smith enters 250 ac in Rockingham Co on waters of Wolf Island Cr; border: on W of William Russel and claimant's own land.

R153. entry withdrawn May 13, 1793. Feb. 28, 1793 Charles Moore enters 40 ac in Rockingham Co on waters of Little Troublesom Cr; border: Robert Barr, William Stratton, & claimant's own line.

R154. entry withdrawn May 13, 1793. Feb. 28, 1793 Charles Moore enters 10 ac in Rockingham Co on Big Troublesom Cr; border: Moses Deen and claimant's own land.

R155. entry withdrawn Jun. 13, 1793. Mar. 16, 1793 William Farrar enters 150 ac in Rockingham Co on S side of Dan R; border: John Oliver, Isaac Whitworth, land lately property of William Hiss desc, & land "I" purchased of Samuel Henderson who purchased of John Whitworth.

R156. Mar. 16, 1793 Pleasant Henderson enters 100 ac in Rockingham Co on W side of Jacobs Cr; border: his own deeded land, Alexander Martin, Robert Martin, & land late property of Robert & John Nelson desc.

R157. Mar. 16, 1793 Peter Oliver enters 100 ac on Piney Br "which Henry Pratt settled" on waters of Upper Hogans Cr; border: W corner of James Oliver's 50 ac, & on E side said branch (includes "all the Platt land").

R158. Mar. 18, 1793 James Hays jr enters 50 ac in Rockingham Co on waters of Jacobs Cr; border: his own land on E side & W line and on N side of Whetston Hill.

R159. withdrawn. Mar. 18, 1793 James Hays jr enters 100 ac in Rockingham Co on Popplar Br of Jacobs Cr; borer: his own [land] on N side and Frederick Ford.

R160. Mar. 18, 1793 Thomas Henderson esq enters 250 ac in Rockingham Co; border: his own [land] & John Barnes on W, Nicholas Larimer, & "perhaps" Col. Alexander Martin.

R161. withdrawn. Mar. 22, 1793 Abraham Philips esq enters 200 ac in Rockingham Co between Glady and Piney Creeks; border: Robert Small, Harston, & Marr's late survey.

R162. Mar. 18, 1793(sic) Abraham Philips esq enters 17 ac on waters of Piney Cr; border: David Moore, William Miller, & Robert Small's late survey.

R163. Mar. 28, 1793 Alexander Sneed enters 200 ac in Rockingham Co on waters of Buffallow Island Cr; border: William Harris and Grogan.

R164. Apr. 13, 1793 Frederick (or Zederick) Ford enters 40 ac in Rockingham Co on waters of Jacobs Cr; border: John Shepperd, George Ford, James Hayes jr, & claimant's own line.

R165. withdrawn. Apr. 20, 1793 Abraham Philips esq and Alexander McClaran enter 200 ac in Rockingham Co on waters of Dan R; border: Roberts, Gallaway, & William Proctor.

R166. withdrawn. Apr. 20, 1793 William Johnson and Alexander McClaran enter 150 ac in Rockingham Co on Moses Cr; border: Joel Walker, Gideon Johnson, Thomas Henderson, & widow Scury.

R167. warrant issued in name of Wm Jones instead of McClaran. Apr. 20, 1793 Andrew Allen and Alexander McClaran enter 300 ac in Rockingham Co on waters of Troublesom Cr; border: George Brown.

R168. withdrawn. Apr. 20, 1793 Robert Pamplion enters 65 ac in Rockingham Co on waters of Town Cr; border: Allumby Williams and Rev. David Caldwell; includes part of Piney Hill.

R169. Apar. 30, 1793 Abraham Philips esq enters 100 ac in Rockingham Co on waters of Troublesom Cr; border: Harston, Marr's late survey, & Robert Small.

R170. withdrawn. Apr. 30, 1793 Alexander McClaran and Abraham Philips esq enters 300 ac in Rockingham Co on waters of Bever Island and Reed Creeks; border or near: John Seales and Jacob Camplin.

R171. May 2, 1793 Gideon Johnson jr enters 100 ac in Rockingham Co on waters of Moses Cr; border: John Caldwell, Susannah Scurry, & claimant's own land.

R172. withdrawn. May 16, 1793 Abraham Philips esq enters 100 ac in Rockingham Co on both sides of Reeds Cr waters of Bullews Cr; border: John McPeek, Cornelious Cook, & Guilford County line.

R173. May 18, 1793 George Hamblin enters 100 ac in Rockingham Co on Upper Hogans Cr; border: William Neal.

R174. May 27, 1793 James Hayes jr enters 150 ac in Rockingham Co on Brushey fork of Jacobs Cr; border: Jacob Whitworth and John Carner; includes Joseph Gormon's improvement.

R175. May 27, 1793 James Oliver enters 100 ac in Rockingham Co on waters of Upper Hogans Cr; border: John Oliver on S side of said creek.

R176. May 28, 1793 Jacob Whitworth sr enters 100 ac in Rockingham Co on waters of Jacobs Cr and on both sides of Brushey fork of Jacobs Cr; border: Isaac Parimon's former land and claimant's own lines.

Rockingham County, NC Land Entries 1790-1795

Book 3

R177. May 31, 1793 Robert Cummings enters 150 ac in Rockingham Co on waters of Haw R; border: Abraham Philips esq and claimant's own land.

R178. May 31, 1793 John Armstrong enters 200 ac in Rockingham Co on head waters of Quarquaw Cr; border: Christopher Dudley, "on" Chork Level, and crossed Sorrow Town road; includes the crossroads.

R179. Jun. 17, 1793 Nathaniel Harris enters 60 ac in Rockingham Co on waters of Matrimoney Cr on S side; border: Deskin Grant and claimant's own land.

R180. withdrawn. Jun. 29, 1793 Abraham Philips esq and Nathaniel Linder enter 100 ac in Rockingham Co on waters of Buffellow Island Cr; border: Mainyard Colley, Desken Grant, & David Alexander.

R181. Jul. 12, 1793 Thomas Grogan enters 130 ac in Rockingham Co on waters of Mayo R; border: Benjamin Smith; includes place Thomas Grogan bought from Charles Gallaway.

R182. Jul. 17, 1793 William Cannon enters 50 ac in Rockingham Co on waters of Jacobs Cr; border: John Shepherd and Jacob Whitworth.

R183. Aug. 3, 1793 Thomas Pounds enters 30 ac in Rockingham Co on waters of Wolf Island Cr; border: Absolem Gootser "or" John Granger.

R184. Aug. 4, 1793 Philip Gales enters 100 ac in Rockingham Co on head waters of Jacobs Cr; border: John Chadwell and his own lines.

R185. warrant issued in name of Cotterall. Aug. 26, 1793 Nathaniel Linder enters 50 ac in Rockingham Co on waters of Upper Hogans Cr; border: Edward Cotteral and Warren Walker desc.

R186. withdrawn. Aug. 29, 1793 Robert Small enters 200 ac in Rockingham Co on waters of Jacobs Cr; border: John Cummings on S & E.

R187. Aug. 30, 1793 William Farrar enters 200 ac in Rockingham Co; border: on W & S by land Farrar bought from John Chadwell.

R188. Sept. 17, 1793 James Lord enters 35 ac; border: John McCarrol; includes "that part" sold David Morris.

R189. Sept. 17, 1793 John Odell esq enters 585 ac in Rockingham Co on both sides of White Oak Cr; border or near: "order line" near road from Purkins' ferry to Richard Marr's.

R190. Sept. 24, 1793 John George enters 40 ac on waters of Bigg Troublesom Cr in Rockingham Co; border: Matthew George.

R191. Oct. 9, 1793 Chesley Barnes enters 40 ac in Rockingham Co on waters of Buffallow Island Cr; border: lines Zachariah King purchased of John Fenden Keer and claiment's old line.

R192. warrant issued to Wm Bethel esq instead of McClaran. Oct. 10, 1793 Abraham Philips esq and Alexander McClaran enter 200 ac in Rockingham Co on waters of Fishing Cr; border: Peter Dunkin and Curtis.

R193. withdrawn. Oct. 15, 1793 Hezekiah Cary and Ephraim Thompson enter 200 ac in Rockingham Co; border: John McPeek's S line.

R194. withdrawn. Oct. 15, 1793 John Odell esq enters 200 ac in Rockingham Co on waters of Wolf Island Cr; border: Boyd, "near" Lavan Down, and John McCabbin.

R195 withdrawn. Oct. 15, 1793 Abraham Philips esq and Alexander McClaran enter 200 ac in Rockingham Co on waters of Burchfield's fork of Wolf Island Cr; border: William Harris and William Adkins.

R196. withdrawn. Oct. 16, 1793 William Jones enters 200 ac in Rockingham Co on both sides of Big road from Purkins ferry.; border: Shurwood Toney's deeded land and Abraham Spencer desc.

R197. issued to Wm Bethell esq instead of A McClaran. Nov. 11, 1793 Abraham Philips esq and Alexander McClaran enter 165 ac in Rockingham Co on waters of Fishing Cr; border: Peter Dunkin, Charles Gallaway, & Curtis.

R198. withdrawn. Nov. 11, 1793 Levin Mitchell enters 300 ac in Rockingham Co on Town Cr; border: Thomas Rafferty and John Young.

R199. Nov. 18, 1793 Reuben Taylor enters 30 ac in Rockingham Co; border: William Boyd, Shurwood Toney, & claiment's own land.
R200. Nov. 20, 1793 Asa Brashears enters 150 ac in Rockingham Co on waters of Jacobs Cr; border: Samuel Short on S and his own tract on E which is called the mill seat.

R201. Nov. 21, 1793 Leven Mitchell enters 409 ac in Rockingham Co on waters of Town Cr; border: Thomas Rafferty and claiment's own land.

R202. Nov. 26, 1793 Chesley Barnes enters 70 ac in Rockingham Co; border: "my" own line "on a white oak".

R203. Nov. 26, 1793 Wyatt Stublefield enters 100 ac in Rockingham Co on waters of Wolf Island Cr; border: his own [land] and Mills.

R204. Nov. 26, 1793 James Wright enters 100 ac in Rockingham Co on waters of Bever Island Cr; border: Col. James Hunter and John Joyce.

R205. Dec. 6, 1793 Thomas Rafferty enters 100 ac in Rockingham Co on waters of Wolf Island Cr; border: Isaac Cantrell jr, William Bethell esq, & Leven Mitchell's late entry.

R206. Dec. 9, 1793 Morris Humphris enters 60 ac in Rockingham Co on waters of Mayo R; border: Virginia line and county line in NW corner of above mentioned county.

R207. Dec. 14, 1793 Isaac Cantrell jr enters 50 ac on waters of Mill Cr; border: his own [land] and Cummings.

R208. Dec. 23, 1793 David Rowland enters 40 ac in Rockingham Co; between Troublesom Cr and Haw R; border: Sprout and claimant's own line.

R209. Jan. 1, 1794 Thomas Knight enters 100 ac in Rockingham Co; border: William Greer and claimant's own line; includes Thomas Simpson's improvement.

R210. Jan. 4, 1794 Moses Short sr enters 50 ac in Rockingham Co on waters of Bigg Troublesom Cr; border: John Cummings, Thomas King, & claimant's own lines.

R211. Jan. 6, 1794 Reuben Tyler enters 50 ac in Rockingham Co; border: William Boyd, Shurwood Toney, & claimant's own line.

R212. Jan. 8, 1794 Abraham Philips esq enters 146 ac on waters of Town Cr; border: Leven Mitchell, John Rafferty, & Robert Hutson.

[R213] 113 (sic). Jan. 11, 1794 Hezekiah Cary and Ephraim Thompson enter 250 ac in Rockingham Co; border: John McPeek's S line and Jacob Philips "or" Kilpatrick.

R214. Jan. 13, 1794 John Brown enters 50 ac in Rockingham Co; border: William Proctor on S & E.

R215. Jan. 13, 1794 Robert Pamplin enters 99 ac in Rockingham Co on waters of Town Cr; border: Allumby Williams, Thomas Rafferty, Cornelious Mabrey sr, & Rev. David Caldwell.

R216. Jan. 14, 1794 Jesse Young enters 100 ac in Rockingham Co on waters of Jacobs Cr; border: William Greer (or Grurs) and James Archer.

R217. Jan. 22, 1794 William Damron enters 250 ac in Rockingham Co on waters of Bellews Cr; border: Prudence Wright.
R218. Jan. 22, 1794 William Damron enters 100 ac in Rockingham Co on waters of Bellews Cr; border: William Kinman and Prudance Wright.

R219. Jan. 27, 1794 William Fenning enters 50 ac in Rockingham Co on waters of Lick fork of Buffellow Island Cr; border: on N side [his] own land.

R220. Feb. 1, 1794 Abraham Philips esq enters 150 ac in Rockingham Co; border: John Armstrong and Sarah Parker on waters of Dan R.

R221. Feb. 8, 1794 John Heath enters 50 ac in Rockingham Co; border: Matthew Pegg on E and Charles Bruce.

R222. Feb. 22, 1794 Joseph Bennet enters 60 ac in Rockingham Co on waters of Bigg Troublesom Cr on N side; border: John Cumming and Thomas King.

R223. Feb. 26, 1794 Almond Given enters 50 ac in Rockingham Co on waters of Upper Hogans Cr; bo;rder: John Kohoon; includes both sides of Bigg road.

R224. Feb. 26, 1794 James Hunter esq enters 100 ac in Rockingham Co on waters of Bever Island Cr; border: claimant's lines, John Joyce, & Samuel Gann.

R225. Mar. 5, 1794 Henry Garnet enters 100 ac in Rockingham Co on waters of Lick fork of Buffellow Island Cr; border: claimant's own line on S and William Fenning on E.

R226. Mar. 14, 1794 William Southerland enters 200 ac in Rockingham Co on waters of Bellews Cr; border: claimant's own line and James Reagan.

R227. Apr. 3, 1794 Charles Baker enters 50 ac in Rockingham Co on waters of Piney Cr; border: Robert Martin, Robert Boak, & claimant's own line.

R228. Apr. 21, 1794 Henry Seales enters 100 ac in Rockingham Co on waters of Buffellow Island Cr; border: his own land and Alexander Sneed.

R229. Apr. 14, 1794 Abraham Philips esq enters 570 ac in Rockingham Co on waters of Dan R on both sides of Curbys Cr; border: Robert Larimer, Francis Fore, John Forguson, & Alexander Martin esq.

R230. Apr. 14, 1794 William Bethell and Abraham Philips esqs enter 200 ac on waters of Dan R; border: John Odell esq's late survey and "Farleys order".

R231. May 3, 1794 Abraham Philips esq enters 100 ac in Rockingham Co; border: his own land, George Pursell and William Jones.

R232. issued in name of James Sanders sr. May 5, 1794 Alexander McClaran enters 40 ac in Rockingham Co on both sides of Brushey fork of Bigg Rockhouse Cr; border: his own land formerly belonging to Miner Mash and James Sanders.

R233. May 6, 1794 John Sanders enters 30 ac in Rockingham Co; border: James Sanders sr and William Jones.

R234. May 12, 1794 Vincent Wheeler enters 200 ac in Rockingham Co on waters of Burchfields fork of Wolf Island Cr; border: William Adkins.

R235. May 21, 1794 Almond Given enters 300 ac in Rockingham Co on waters of Upper Hogans Cr; border: Alexander Martin esq, Charles Bruce, John Forguson, tract that Edward Cotteral lives on, & [his] own 50 ac entry.

R236. May 23, 1794 Thomas Rafferty enters 126 ac in Rockingham Co; border: Isaac Cantrell jr, Leven Mitchell, & claimant's own land.

R237. May 27, 1794 Francis Wright enters 100 ac in Rockingham Co; border: Edward Stublefield, Tiblitha Browder, John Linder, & William Bethell esq.

R238. issued in name of Vincent Wheeler. May 28, 1794 Alexander McClaran enters 150 ac in Rockingham Co on waters of Upper Hogans Cr; border: W of and joins Sarah Kirkpatrick.

R239. May 30, 1794 Robert Means enters 50 ac in Rockingham Co; border: William Reddles corner and Samuel Sharp.

R240. Jun. 2, 1794 Richard Smith enters 100 ac in Rockingham Co on Londons or Stoney Cr; border: Reuben Tyler, Bloyd, & on both sides of a branch.

R241. Jun. 30, 1794 Alexander Joyce enters 100 ac in Rockingham Co; border: William Motley's corner, Matthew Pegg, John Dale, & James Edwards.

R242. Jun. 30, 1794 Alexander Joyce enters 65 ac in Rockingham Co; border: William Blake's corner, Champ Gibson, & William Riddle.

R243. Jul. 17, 1794 Alexander Joyce 50 ac in Rockingham Co on waters of Jacobs Cr; border: Thomas Lowe and Robert Nelson desc.

R244. Aug. 12, 1794 William Young enters 100 ac in Rockingham Co on W side of Hogans Cr; border: Charles Bruce and William Neel.

R245. issued in name of Gideon Johnson jr. Aug. 20, 1794 Alexander McClaran enters 200 ac in Rockingham Co on S side of Dan R; border: lands entered by Col. James Martin and Gideon Johnson jr's late entry.

R246. Aug. 21, 1794 Alexander Joyce enters 50 ac in Rockingham Co; border: Jacob Barnet and Jacob Cantrell.

R247. Sept. 14, 1794 William Howard enters 166 ac in Rockingham Co on waters of Moses Cr; border: Ely Scurry desc, Elmore Walker sr, Thomas Henderson esq, Joel Walker, & Gideon Johnson.

R248. Oct. 16, 1794 Hezekiah Cary enters 80 ac in Rockingham Co on N side of Burges Stone between "that" and Lewis Peoples and widow Trotters.

R249. Oct. 20, 1794 John Stockard enters 65 ac in Rockingham Co on waters of Jacobs Cr; border: William Yours on N, James Wright on E, & his own land on S & W.

R250. Nov. 17, 1794 James Roach enters 100 ac in Rockingham Co on waters of Little Rockhouse Cr; border: John McKenney and Robertson Ross.

R251. Nov. 12, 1794 Joseph Odell enters 100 ac in Rockingham Co on waters of Mayo R; border: James Rhoads on S and Ansel Fields on N.

R252. Nov. 20, 1794 Joseph Odell enters 50 ac in Rockingham Co; border: deeded land "where I now live the upper corner on N".

R253. Nov. 20, 1794 Alexander McClaran enters 100 ac in Rockingham Co on waters of Buffellow Island Cr; border: Reece Price and Christopher Hand.

R254. Nov. 20, 1794 Alexander McClaran enters 50 ac in Rockingham Co on waters of Lick fork of Buffelellow Island Cr; border: Henry Powers on N.

R255. Nov. 26, 1794 James Grant enters 100 ac in Rockingham Co; between John Mount sr, William Russel, Richard Marr, & John Jones.

R256. Dec. 4, 1794 Nathaniel Dodd enters 200 ac in Rockingham Co on waters of Mayo R; border: Allen Dodd's S line and George Deathridge jr's N line.

R257. Dec. 26, 1794 Nathaniel Linder enters 100 ac in Rockingham Co on waters of Jacobs Cr; border: John Howel on "W line at a post oak his corner" and Robert Rolston.

R258. Jan. 3, 1795 Clabon Wall enters 10 ac in Rockingham Co; between Aaron Williams desc, Robert Galloway & Co, Daniel Wall sr, & John Wall.

R259. Jan. 13, 1795 Hezekiah Cary enters 100 ac in Rockingham Co at head of Kings Br; "at my corner and Ephraim Thompson's".

R260. Jan. 13, 1795 Hezekiah Cary enters 79 ac in Rockingham Co; border: William Greer.

R261. Jan. 20, 1795 John Oliver enters 60 ac in Rockingham Co on waters of Dan R; border: a late entry of Robert Gains; between Isaac Whitworth, Thomas Henarson(?), Robert Gillaland, & "my" own land.

R262. Jan. 21, 1795 Alexander McClaran enters 400 ac in Rockingham Co on waters of Jacobs Cr and Troublesom Cr; border: entry Hezekiah Cary made on N of Burgis Stone.

R263. Jan. 30, 1795 James Thomas enters 50 ac in Rockingham Co on waters of Upper Hogans Cr; between deeded land of John Adkerson and Charles Bruce.

R264. Jan. 30, 1795 John Hunter enters 100 ac in Rockingham Co on waters of Wide Mouth Cr and Rockey Br of Dan R; border: on N by "Farleys Order", on S by Shurwood Toney & Gunter's former tract, & on E by survey lately made for William Bethell esq, John Odell, & Joshua Shoemake.

R265. Jan. 30, 1795 William Dearing enters 300 ac in Rockingham Co on SE side of Dan R; border: his own lines, Adam Crafford, Isaac Whitworth, & widow Stephens.

Above books compared with original entrys and certified to be correct by A Philips JP and R Callaway JP.

Rockingham Co, NC Jun. 15, 1796 In obedience to an act of the Assembly all entry takers books (since formation of the county) have been "called" with names of entry takers and their securities; the books have been copied and compared with the originals; the results are books 1, 2, and 3; entry takers

were/are: (a) William Clark esq, former entry taker, and his security Joseph Clark esq and (b) Alexander McClaran, present entry taker, and his security Abraham Philips esq.   Signed William Bethell cc.
END OF BOOK

Barnes, John   R160
Barnet, David   R139
Barnet, Jacob   2310, R246
Barnet, Thimothey   2553
Barnet (Barnett), William
    2114, 2494
Barnett, Benjamin   2681
Barnett, Luke   2351
Barney, Charles   2465
Barnhardt (Barnhart), Henry
    1865, 2016, 2451
Barns, James   2137
Barr, James   1886, 1978, 2232
Barr, Robert   1979, R153
Barronhill, William   2256
Barrow, Moses   2401, R134
Barrow, Philip   2717
Beaely, John   2564
Beal, John jr   2379
Beal (Beall), Thaddeus   1916,
    2119
Beall, Joseph B   2070
Beall, Thaddens   1959
Beals, William   2379
Beard, George   2439
Beard, Richard   2439
Beard, William   1940, 1947
Beason (Beeson), Isaac   2166,
    2307, 2338, 2372, 2425
Beason, Mary   2457
Belgg, Claeb   2110
Bell,   2785
Bell, Francis   2149
Bell, John   2104, 2131
Bell, Joseph   2070
Bell, Samuel   2149
Bell, Thaddeus (Thadues)
    2325, 2771, 2772
Bell, Thomas   2183
Benaman,   2167
Benbow,   2682
Benbow, Thomas   2431
Bennet, Joseph   R222
Bennett (Bennit), Elisha   2546,

2704
Benson, John   2650
Bernard, Luke   R111
Bethel, Samuel   2461
Bethell (Bethel), William
    1885, 1923, 2088, 2461,
    R97, R143, R144, R192,
    R197, R205, R230, R237,
    R264, R265
Bignm, Thomas   2701
Billingsley, Henry   2697
Billingsly, James   2301
Bingham, Thomas   2786
Black, Thomas   2264, 2776
Blackburn, John   R104
Blackley, Robert   1949, 1958,
    2007
Blagg, Calebb   2641
Blair, Joseph   1863
Blake, William   R242
Blakley,   1950
Blankeny, Robert   1921
Bloyd,   R240
Boak, Robert   R129, R227
Bobbit, Isham   1876
Bond, Edward   2304
Bond, John   2379
Boon, Jacob   2242, 2456, 2524
Boon, John   1942, 1969
Borrow, Philip   2533
Bostick, William   1856, 2026
Bowen, Benjamin   2071
Bowen, John   R106, R107
Bowen, Thomas   2071, 2168
Bowman,   2784
Boyd,   1896, 2161
Boyd, Ann   2933
Boyd, James   2500
Boyd, Nathaniel   2492, 2709
Boyd,   R194
Boyd, William   R199, R211
Braden, Alexr   2538
Braden, Charles   2221
Bradford,   2552, 2601

Burney, Charles   2467
Burney, William   2551, 2555
Burns, Patrick   2120, 2121
Burrow, Jarrald   2580
Burrow, Philip   2772, 2781
Burrow, Philip jr   2769
Burrow, Philip sr   2769
Busey, Thos   1977
Busis, Thomas   2676
Butle, James   2297
Caffey, Michael   2394, R108
Caffy, Michael   2488
Calaham, Darby   2094
Caldwell,   1981, 2739
Caldwell, Alexander   1949,
  1950, 2007, 2252, 2275,
  2408
Caldwell, David   2272, 2310,
  2526, 2540, 2653, 2940,
  R137, R168, R215
Caldwell, Doctor   2753
Caldwell (Calwell), James
  2188, 2784
Caldwell, John   R102, R171
Caldwell, Richard   2180
Calhoon,   2078
Call, Robert   2310
Callahan, William   R121
Callaway, R   R265
Callums, William   R105
Campbell, James   1946, 1947,
  1956, 2163
Campbell (Campbel), John
  2224, 2573
Campbell, Moses   2390
Camplin, Henry   2729, 2764
Camplin, Jacob   R170
Camplin, James   2953
Canaday (Canady), John   2260,
  2275
Canaday (Canady), Joseph
  2275, 2560
Canady, Charles   1926
Cannon, Minos   2137, 2273,

2279, 2383
Cannon, William   R182
Cantrell, Isaac   2283, 2481
Cantrell, Isaac jr   R205. R207,
  R236
Cantrell (Cantel), Jacob   2282,
  R246
Cantrell, John   2286
Cantril,   2276
Caple, Philip   2524
Cardwell, Richard   R105
Cardwell, Rick P   1919
Carey, Arthur   2311
Carmichael (Carmichal),
  Andrew   2235, 2693, 2745,
  2755, 2911
Carnahan, John   2536
Carner, John   R174
Carner, John D   2491
Carners, John   R114
Carney, Arthur   2122
Carrick, widow   2765
Carringer, Andrew   2477
Carrol, Cain   1900
Carron, George   1890
Carruthers, James   1902, 2000
Carsey, widow   2366
Cartary, William   2465
Carter, George   2489
Carter, Giles   2225
Carter, Thomas   2294, R125
Caruthers, Martha   2000
Cary (Carry), Hezekiah   R106,
  R107, R193, R213, R248,
  R259, R260, R262
Casey, Samuel   2683, 2702
Castle, George   1902
Caswell, Richard   2790
Caswell, widow   2554
Causbey, James   2730
Cawhoon, Samuel   2168
Cawsey, Thomas   2668
Chadlas, Hugh   2156
Chadwell, John   R118, R119,

R184, R187

Challis (Callus), Hugh   2154, 2184

Chambers, Henry   2146, 2148

Chambers, John   2141

Chambers, Thomas   R144

Chapman, Joseph   2411

Chappel, Ambrose   2467

Charles, Elijah   1977, 2328, 2450

Charles, Elisha   2530

Charles, Leven   2005

Charles, William   2482

Chassir, Joseph   1974

Chilcart, John   2176

Chilint, John   1954

Chrestshlaw, James   2462

Chrisman, Abraham   2926

Chrisman, George   2611

Chrisman, Jacob   2459

Christman, Jacob   2673

Clap,   2785

Clapp, Adam   2478

Clapp, Andrew   2477

Clapp (Clap), George   2261, 2708, 2735

Clapp, Glass   2270

Clapp, Jacob   2684

Clapp (Clap), John P   1859, 1945, 2270, 2772

Clapp (Clap), Lodwick (Lodiwick)   2261, 2657, 2769, 2770, 2772

Clapp (Clap), Tobias   2261, 2324, 2546, 2579, 2618, 2657

Clark, John   1943, 2388, 2389, 2791, 2792

Clark, Joseph   R265

Clark, Thomas   1922

Clark, William   1870, 1871, 1941, 1942, R119, R265

Clark, William jr   2054

Clerk, Hance   2454

Clow, David   2016

Cobb (Cob), Henry   2091, 2278, 2528

Coble,   1945

Coble, George   1905, 1945, 2259, 2332

Coble, John   2735

Coble, Nichles   2765, 2777

Coble, Philip   2455

Cobler, Ctrustdc   2371

Cobler, Frederick   2371

Coe, John   2886

Coeble, Jacob   2890

Coffin, Bethuel (Bethewel)   2289, 2363

Coffin, Levi   2540, 2945

Coffin, Matthew (Mathew)   2399, 2402, 2450, 2689, 2727, 2737, 2747, 2848

Colbreath, Alexr   2374

Colley (Collsy), Mainyard (Minerd)   R123, R180

Colson,   2026

Colston, Henry   2496

Conn, John   2394

Conner, Andrew   2317

Cook, Abraham   2307, 2338, 2425

Cook, Cornelius (Cornelious)   2002, 2033, 2962, R172

Cook, Hery   2963

Cook, John   2661

Cook, Reuben   2040

Cook, William jr   R89

Cooper, David   1859

Cooper, John   2227, 2935

Coots, James   2125, 2140, 2567

Coots, John   2593

Copelin, Hugh   1985

Copelin, John   1985, 2584

Cornet, Jacob   2263

Corry, Robert   1896

Cortner, George   2691, 2790

Dent,   2769
Dent, Peter   2508, 2741
Dent, William   1982, 1983,
    2027, 2044, 2119, 2130,
    2323, 2325, 2518, 2781,
    2790
Dent, William jr   1937, 2304
Denton, Samuel   2067, 2146
Devalt, Jacob   2045
Devenney (Deveny, Diviney),
    Samuel   1985, 2584, 2686
Deweace, Ezekiel   2692
Dewing, Robert   1895, 2098
Diamond, Patrick   2534, 2535,

    2536, 2654
Diamond, Steward   2534
Diamond, William   2254,
    2654, 2697
Dick, Peter   1941
Dick, William   1982, 2163
Dick, widow   1898
Dicker (Dickies), Peter   2379
Dickey, James   2501, 2744,
    2745
Dickey (Dickies), William
    2099, 2380, 2562, 2635,
    2744, 2832
Dickson, William   2535, 2536,
    2633
Dill, Fredk   2390
Dill, James   2332
Dillion, Peter   1869
Dillon (Dillin), Daniel   1953,
    1958, 1981, 2538, 2642
Dillon, Daniel jr   2581
Dillon (Dillan), Jesse   2887,
    2954
Dillon (Dillin), Nathan   1950,
    1953, 1958, 1981, 1984,
    2074, 2187, 2393, 2642
Dillon (Dillin), William   2251,
    2329, 2592, 2949
Dilworth, widow   2031

Dinnis, Isaac   2097
Dishorn, Aaron   2721
Dixon, William   2573, 2694
Dixon, widow   2032
Dobion, Joseph   2235
Dobsin,   2562
Dobson, John   2693
Dobson, Joseph   2100
Dobson, Wm   2613
Dodd, Allen   R256
Dodd, Nathaniel   R256
Dodson, Lambath   1880
Dollon, Samuel   2150
Dollson, Lambert   2018
Donn, William   1858
Donnel, Andrew   2941
Donnel, George   2467
Donnel, James   1927, 2758
Donnel, Thomas   1872
Donnell,   2778
Donnell, Wm   2608
Donnill, John   2221
Donnol,   1872
Dorres, Isaac   2088
Dortherty, Daniel   2538
Dotton,   2058
Dotton, Samuel sr   2174
Dottson, Lambert   2018
Douglas, David   2210, 2212
Down, Lavan   R194
Downey, William   2733, 2759
Drick, Samuel   2359
Driskil, Eli A   2713
Duck, Samuel   2407, 2409
Dudley, Christopher   R178
Duest, Ezekiel   2692
Duff, John   2161
Duff, William   1883
Dun, Frederick   2166
Dun, Joshua   2715, 2716
Dunkin, Peter   R192, R197
During, John   1882
Duskey, George   2687
Duvcast, Ezekiel   2692

2523
Foney, Sherwood 2356
Forbes (Forbus), Arthur 2246,
  2329, 2592
Forbes, Elizabeth 2557
Forbes (Forbies), George
  2560, 2590, 2895
Forbes, Hugh 2542, 2702
Forbes, Jno 2575
Forbush, Betty 2752
Forbush, Elizabeth 2557
Forbush, George 2560, 2590
Forbush, Hugh 2542
Forbush, John 2638, 2751
Ford, Frederick R159, R164
Ford, George R164
Ford, Henry 2214, 2252, 2314
Ford, Zederick R164
Fore, Francis R229
Fore, Peter 2330
Forguson, Allexander 2675
Forguson (Forgeson), John
  2262, 2401, R229, R235
Forster, Hugh 2793
Foster, John 1870, 1871,
  1986, 1987, 2599
Foster, William 1983
Foton, 2400
Foud, Christian 2048
Four, Francis R124
Foust, John 2546
Fowler, William 2032
Fowmy, Dennis 2523
Franlkner, John 2334
Frazer, 2556
Frazer, Isaac 2966
Frazer, James 1951, 1987,
  2248, 2255, 2405, 2412
Frazer, John 2929
Frazer (Frasher), Samuel
  1939, 2250, 2398, 2429,
  2514, 2545, 2783
Freland, James 2145
Frohock, 1915, 2140, 2182

Frohock, Thomas 2258
Frost, Jonas 2203, R104
Frotter, Ephraim 2934
Fruman, Wm 1911
Fulkson, 2254
Fulton, Daniel 2425
Fulton (Fulten), Samuel 1970,
  2426, 2614, 2663, 2726
Gains, Robert 2498, R261
Galbreath, Alexander 1866
Galbreath (Galbraith), Robert
  2289, 2363, 2365, 2700
Gales, Philip R184
Galey, widow 2263
Gallaway, R165
Gallaway (Galloway), Charles
  1960, 2240, 2241, R138,
  R181, R197
Galloway, Robert R258
Gamble, William 1905, 2270,
  2325, 2893
Gambol, Andrew 2560
Gann, John 2175
Gann, Samuel R224
Gansel, 2378
Gardner, 2521
Gardner, Isaac 2537
Gardner, James 2663
Gardner, Silvanus 2589
Gardner (Garner), Stephen
  2207, 2208, 2511, 2537,
  2667
Gardner, Stephen B 2513
Gardner, William 1976, 2545,
  2764
Garinger, Andrew 2477, 2478
Garinger (Garginger), Basten
  (Boston) 2072, 2455, 2456,
  2672
Garner, Thomas 2008
Garnet, Henry R225
Garrel (Garrell), Ralph 1908,
  2264, 2505, 2805
Gaster, 2776

Graus,   2750
Gray, Alexander   1922, 2170
Gray, Alexander jr   2950
Gray, Andrew   2422, 2492
Gray, Leven   2447
Gray, William   1917, 2035,
   2425, 2441
Greddlebough, Thomas   2549
Gree, Alexander   2102
Green, Henry   2789
Green, James   2122
Green, Robert   2260, 2275
Green, Sarah   2354
Green, Thomas   1916
Green (Greens), William
   2789, 2881
Greer,   2705
Greer, William   2272, R209,
   R216, R260
Greeson,   2769
Greson, Isaac   2703
Grier, Willm   2640
Grim, Almon   1882
Grogan,   2058
Grogan, Bartholomew   2416
Grogan, Henry   2199, 2371
Grogan,   R163
Grogan, Thomas   1997, 2059,
   R181
Grun, widow   2459
Grunger, John   2276
Grunway, Jacob   1931
Grurs, William   R216
Gruson,   2769
Guess (Gruss), John   1962,
   1993, 2089
Gullaspie, Col.   2713
Gullett, Joseph   2778
Gun, Joseph   2434
Guner, John   2147
Gunter, Joel   2362
Gunter,   R264
Gurdens, James   2188
Gwin, Hugh   2298

Hackey, Conrade   2714
Haga, Conrod   2691
Hailey, John   2457
Hains, John   R148
Hairgroves (Hairgrove),
   Benjamin   2035, 2432, 2441
Haley, John (J)   1940, 1977,
   2202, 2482, 2622, 2659,
   2819
Hall, Andrew   1956, 2392
Hall, John   1871, 1986, 1987,
   2245, 2255, 2355, 2599,
   2797
Hall, William   2298, 2406
Hamer, John   2319
Hamilton,   2507
Hamilton, David   1968, 2025
Hamilton, George   2651, 2845
Hamilton, Hance   2299, 2300,
   2302, 2303, 2597, 2634,
   2790, 2795, 2831
Hamilton, J   2659, 2793
Hamilton, James 1952
Hamilton, John   1917, 2132,
   2133, 2134, 2136, 2307,
   2397, 2425, 2502, 2512,
   2513, 2622, 2634, 2790,
   2819, 2831
Hamilton, Matthew   2113,
   2724
Hamilton, Non   2130
Hamilton, Thomas   2115, 2472
Hamilton, Thomas jr   2236
Hamilton, William   2221
Hamlin, George   R173
Hammond, Jesse   1961
Hancock, John   1946
Hand, Christopher   R253
Hanes, Charles   1973
Hanes, Hugh   1979
Hanes, Thomas   1980
Hanes, widow   1995
Haney, Brigdale   2152, 2153
Hannah, Joshua   1856

Harne, John   2319
Harpen, Thomas 2841
Harper, John   2009, 2419
Harper, Thomas   2646
Harris, Evan   2442, 2452
Harris, Nathaniel   R179
Harris, Obadiah   2312
Harris, Peter   2361, 2631
Harris, Robert   2266
Harris, Thompson   2075
Harris, William   R163, R195
Harrison, Nathaniel   2037
Harrison, William   2288
Harry, John   1925, 2137
Harston,   R161, R169
Hart, Henry   2419, 2456, 2617
Hartgrave, Samuel   2358, 2530
Hartgrove, widow   2508
Hartgroves, Benj   2420
Harvel, John   2741
Harver, Richd   2093
Harvey, Sipple   2908
Haskins, John   1916
Hatfield, Samuel   2139
Hawel, John   2667
Hawkins (Hawkings),
   2579, 2655
Hawkins, John   2422, 2435,
   2546, 2661
Hawkins, Mary   2579
Hawkins, widow   2690
Haworth, Georg   2952
Hay,   2051
Hays, James   1861, 2068,
   2132, 2133, 2254, 2349,
   2350
Hays (Hayes), James jr   R158,
   R159, R164, R174
Hays (Hayes), James sr   R114
Hays, John   2654
Hays, Thomas   2030, 2480
Hayward, Gardner   2209
Hayward, Stephen   2209
Healey, John   1977, 2202,

2339, 2340, 2373, 2585,
   2676
Healy,   2582
Healy, John   2587
Heath, John   R221
Heatt, Christopher jr   2545
Heckman, George   2826
Hedgcock, Joshua   2548
Hellan, James   2186
Helms, John   1896
Helton, James   2434, 2619
Helton, Peter   2434
Helton, Wm   2619
Henarson, Thomas   R261
Henderson,   2107
Henderson, Archer B   2107
Henderson, James   1904, 2306,
   2471, 2487, 2547
Henderson, Michael   2105,
   2518
Henderson, Pleasant   R114,
   R156
Henderson, Richard   2082
Henderson, Samuel   2185,
   R155
Henderson, Thomas   1894,
   2132, 2133, 2134, 2307,
   2370, 2395, 2425, 2527,
   2543, R112, R113, R119,
   R139, R151, R160, R166,
   R247
Herbing, John   2164
Herd, Henry   2671
Hermon, Ephraim   2787, 2790,
   2882
Herren, Samuel   R148
Herrin, Owen   2374
Hichins, Drury   1892
Hickman, William   2755
Hiett (Hyatt),   2763
Hiett (Hyatt), Ashur   2947
Hiett (Hiatt, Hiet, Hyatt),
   George   2293, 2296, 2439,
   2556

Hiett (Hiatt), George jr   2729
Hiett (Heitt, Hiot), Isaac   2188
Hiett (Hyat), Joel   2932
Hiett (Hiatt, Hyatt), John   2495,
2650, 2677
Hiett (Hyatt), Joseph   2366,
2367, 2502
Hiett, William   2427
Hietts, Christopher   2729
Higot, John   2711
Hill, John   R123
Hill, Walter   2423
Hill, Wm   1855
Hilton, Wiliam   2816
Hindman, William   1915
Hinslett, John   2301
Hiss, William   R155
Hitchcock (Hichcok), John
2549, 2646, 2747, 2965
Hitchcock (Hichcok), Joshua
2471, 2549, 2646
Hitchcock, William   2897
Hitton, John   2544
Hocke, widow   2109
Hodges,   R115
Hodges (Hodge), James   R90
Hodges (Hodge), John   1858,
2326, R90
Hodgin, George   2754
Hodgin (Hodgins), John   2410,
2723
Hodson,   2779
Hodson, David   2604, 2630
Hodson, John   2665
Hodson, Jonathan   2630, 2827
Hoggard,   1962
Hoggard, Benjamin   2003,
2014
Hoggatt, David   2762
Hoggatt, Joseph   2445, 2450,
2473
Hoggatt, Nathaniel   2415
Hoggatt, Philip   2700
Hoggatt, William   2571

Hoggatt, widow   2056
Holgan, Thomas   2394
Holiday (Holladay), John
2078, 2169
Holker, Adam   2185
Holland, Edward   2124
Holland, Mary   2711
Holton, Isaac   2513
Hood, John   2550, 2634
Hopewell, James   R94
Hopkins, Caleb   2193
Hopkins, Daniel   2421
Hopkins, David   2128, 2200
Hopkins, Thomas 2722
Horney, John   2188
Horney, Patrick   2413
Horney, William   2358
Hoskins (Hoskin), Arnold
2363, 2365, 2700
Hoskins, John   2197
Hoskins, Joseph   2361
Hough, William   2005
Houlton, Isaac   2110
Howard, Richard   1965
Howard, William   R247
Howel, Jacob   1930
Howel (Howell), John   2537,
2741, 2862, R257
Howel, Jonathan   2413, 2512
Hubbard, John   2730, 2851
Hubbard, Mary 2489
Hudson, David   2802
Hughes, Archibald   1878
Huley, John   2445
Hull, Andrew   1910
Humphris, Morris   R206
Huner, John   2594
Hunt, Abner   2376, 2793
Hunt, Asa (Assa)   2293, 2427,
2440, 2556
Hunt, Eleaner   1899
Hunt, Eleazer   2440
Hunt, Isham   2793
Hunt, Jacob   2389, 2510,

Lanier, James   2334
Lanier, Nathaniel   R180, 2334
Larance, George   2009
Larimer, Nicholas   2498, R160
Larimer, Robert   R124, R229
Larkin,   2139
Larkin, John   2243, 2551, 2554, 2555
Lashley, John   1965
Law, Andrew   2019, 2200, 2342, 2722
Law, Samuel   2062
Lawrance, Adam   2016
Lawrance, George   2419
Lay, James   2319
Layton, Roger   2771, 2786, 2878
Leaper, James   2376
Leister, James   2915
Lellie, Robert   R128
Lenager, Isaac   2306
Leonard,   2607
Leonard, John   2576, 2740, 2774
Leonard, Joseph   2774
Leonard, William   2443
Lephew, Stephen   2241
Leslie, William   2323
Lett, Thomas D   2660
Lewel, Charles   2029
Lewis, John   2411
Lewis, Peter   1923, 2461
Lewis, Richard   1918, 1921, 2138
Lewis, Shadrak   R113
Liester, William   2322
Limebury, George   2734
Linagar, Isaac   2659
Lincey, Thomas   2301, 2302
Linch, Hugh   2066, R127, R129
Linches, Hugh   R108
Linder, John   2466, 2481, R237

Linder, Nathaniel   2391, R93, R109, R141, R142, R149, R150, R185, R257
Linders, John   R94
Lindsey, Robert   2529, 2530
Linegar, Isaac   2341
Liner, John   2285
Liniger, Isaac   2471, 2474
Linsbery, Frances   2027
Linsey, Thomas   2299, 2303
Linsichum, Richard   2779
Linsy, Thos   2300
Linvil,   2107
Linvill (Linvel), David   2103, 2518
Linvill, William   2516
Little, Col.   2268
Little, David   2043
Little, Josiah   R89
Lodowick,   1969
Lodwick, Philip   2671, 2673
Loftis, Job   2155
Loid, Humphrey   2636
Lomax, Thomas   2352
Lomax, William   2112
London, Mark   2129, 2129, 2157
Long, Edward   1906, 1985, 2584
Lonoon, Mark   1888
Lord, James   2288, R188
Louh, David sr   2708
Lour, Davis   1930
Love,   1932
Love, David   2614
Love, Davis   1930
Lovel, David   2217, 2218, 2219, 2220, 2362, R125
Lovel, Jn   2218
Lovel, Joseph   2305
Lovet,   2596
Low,   2769
Low, David   2703, 2704
Low, Isaac   2417

Mayben, David 2905
Mayben, William 2905
Mayon, 2342
Mays, Matthew 2729
Mays, William 1967
McAdow, James 2608, 2806
McAdow, John 2287, 2406,
2509, 2572, 2566, 2577,
2600, 2798
McAlhatan, William 2592
McBride, Francis 2268, 2269,
2334, 2608, 2778
McBride, John 1859, 2127,
2259, 2467, 2564, 2577,
2601, 2799
McBride, John sr 2259
McBride, Josiah 1912
McCabbin, John 2129, R194
McCain, H 2911, 2936, 2969
McCaistions, Moses 2464
McCaleb, Catherine 2760
McCalep, Jean 2760
McCalep, John 2760
McCambler, 2064
McCanes, 2265
McCarrel (McCarrol,
McCarrill, McConill), John
2037, 2108, R188
McCarrel, John jr 2039
McCarrell, John jr 2288
McCarrie, John R92
McClain, John 2746, 2867,
2451
McClaran (McClarans),
Alexander 2395, R102,
R117, R137, R138, R165,
R166, R167, R170, R192,
R195, R197, R232, R238,
R245, R253, R254, R262,
R265
McClean, John 2080
McClean, Joseph 2239
McClellen, James 2158
McClintoch, 2639

McClintock (McClintick), John
2232, 2386, 2595, 2626
McClintock, John J 2626
McCloud, Daniel 1946
McCloud, David 2001
McCollister, Sutton 2437
McCollum (McCollm,
McColm), Barnabas 2501,
2745, 2787
McComb, Jesse 1865, 2451,
2746, 2920
McCommay, Nathaniel 2519
McConney, John 2220
McCoy, John 1894, 1947,
2101, 2527
McCuishim, James 2592
McCuistion (McCuiston),
James 2124, 2249, 2257,
2303, 2329, 2407, 2601
McCulloch, Joseph R115
McCullock, 1945
McCullock, Henry E 2010
McCullock, Henry H 2658
McCullock (McCulloch),
Thomas 1858, 2072, 2081,
2635
McCullum, James 2239
McCurrel, John 2104
McCurry (McCurrey), John
2650, 2727
McCuttum, James 2239
McDill, 2259
McDill, Samuel 2465
McDonnels, John 1884
McDowel, Joseph 2359
McElhatten, 2257
McElhatten, Abraham 2264,
2615
McElroy, John 2529
McFadyens, Jeremih 2126
McGamcery, 2639
McGibbony (McGibeney),
Patrick 2728, 2849
McGlamey, Edward 2232

McGlammary, Edward   2243
McGrady, James   2093, 2251, 2470
McGrady, William   2470
McGuady, James   2364
McHoggard,   1962
McKaige, John   2565
McKain, Hance   2918
McKee, John   2039
McKeen, Alexander   2596, 2790, 2793, 2836
McKenney, John   R250
McKibbin, John   1956, 2064, 2163
McKimic, John   1860
McKimie (McKimic), James   1861, 2194
McKimie, Robert   2160
McKinny, John   2240
McKnight,   2707
McKnny, George   2884
McMical, Archabald   2636, 2631
McMin, Daniel   2575, 2616, 2813
McMullin, John   2683, 2702
McMurry, John   2707
McPeek (McPeak), John   2064, R172, R193, R213
McTeer,   1896
Meacy, Joseph   2745
Means, Robert   2150, 2151, R239
Mebin, William   2628
Mecks, John   2633
Medcalf, James   2430
Meek, John   2621
Meglamery, Edward   1886
Mendinall, Elijah   1975
Mendingall,   2582
Mendingall (Mendenhall, Mendinghall), Aaron   1943, 1965, 2388, 2510, 2517, 2792

Mendingall, Elisha   2458, 2725
Mendingall (Mendenall, Mendinghall), George   2381, 2506, 2507, 2622, 2641, 2666, 2667, 2679, 2705
Mendingall (Mendinghall), James   2450, 2381
Mendingall (Mendinghall), John   2622, 2650
Mendingall, Mary   2358
Mendingall (Mendinghall), Moses   2224, 2606
Mendingall, Phbe   2430
Mendinghall, Mordica (Mardicah)   2620, 2817
Menew, Robert   2578
Meroney, William   2425, 2426
Merrel, Benjamin   2606, 2737, 2804
Merrew, Robert   2578
Meter,   2064
Mileham, Samuel   2621
Mileham, Valintine (Volintine)   2621, 2692, 2818
Mileham, Walter   2694
Miller, Edward   2505
Miller, Joseph   2338
Miller, William   2003, 2003, 2012, 2089, 2292, R98, R146, R162
Millis, Edward   2412, 2743, 2864
Millis, James   2505
Mills, Amos   2344
Mills, Augustus   2199
Mills, Edward   2552
Mills, Hier   2360
Mills, Matthew   2157, 2184
Mills,   R203
Mills, Thomas   2344
Mills, William   R105
Milun, William   2566
Mimsum, Joseph   2516
Mines, John   R135

2326, 2230, 2298, 2327,
2387, 2417, 2460, R90, R115
Pealey, Robert   2531
Peargram, Edward   2891
Pearson, George   1856
Peasley, Col.   2714
Peasley, John   2691
Peasley, Robert   1857, 1924,
1931, 2116, 2145
Peasley, Willm   2683
Peay, George   2055, R99
Peeples, David   1920, 2021,
2189, 2491
Peeples, Drury   2376
Peeples (Peoples), Lewis
2385, R248
Peeples, Nathan (Nathal)
1920, 2021, 2361
Pegg, Martin   2420, 2441,
2543
Pegg, Matthew   R105, R221,
R241
Pegg, Valintine   2527
Peirpont, Larkin   1923
Pendergrass, Luke   2760
Pentell, John   2131
Peoples, Nathaniel   2885
Peorry, John   2331
Periman,   1890
Periman (Perryman), Isaac
1890, 2424
Perkins, Constant   2308
Perkins, Constantine   1961
Perkins, Joseph   1984, 2470,
2517
Perrison, William   2166
Perry, John   2402
Perry, Samuel   2182
Person,   2378
Person, George   2452
Person, James   2739
Person, Thomas   2227
Philips, Abraham   2012, 2036,
2037, 2075, 2082, 2157,

2233, 2319, R117, R134,
R161, R162, R165, R169,
R170, R172, R177, R180,
R192, R195, R197, R212,
R220, R229, R230, R231,
R265
Philips (Philip), Isaac   2038,
2152
Philips, Jacob   2320, R213
Phips, John   2332
Pidgeon, widow   2444
Pierce, George   2028
Pierce, Robert   2553
Pierce, Thomas   1939
Pierpont,   2139
Pinble, John   2039
Pirkins, Joseph   2074, 2187,
2251
Pirkle, John   2104, 2391
Pitts, Henry   2453, 2544
Plumley (Plumbley), William
1963, 2032
Plunket, Thomas   2655, 2708
Plunket (Plunkett, Plunkit),
William   2062, 2081, 2353,
2704
Pope, Charles   2166
Pope, George   2566
Porter, Henry   2305, 2405
Porter, James   2749, 2870
Porter, Joseph   R126
Porter, Mary   2268
Porter, Rees   2102
Porton, Jeremiah   2034, 2097
Potter, Joseph   2362
Potter, Sarah   2217
Pounds, Thomas   R183
Powel, Sampson   2643
Powen, Benjamin   2065
Powers, Henry   R254
Powers, Jesse   2518
Pratt, Henry   R103, R157
Price, Reece   R253
Pritchet, John   2163

Roper, Thomas   2186
Roper, William   2186
Ros, John   2400
Rose, Samuel   2083
Rosen, John   2425, 2426
Ross,   2721
Ross, Henry 2598
Ross, Robertson   R250
Rowland, David   R208
Ruckman, Joseph   2538
Rue, Thomas   2553
Rueses, William   1915
Rukey, John   1866
Rumley (Rumbley), Joseph
  2722, 2751, 2752
Rumley, Smith   2499
Rusing, John   1928
Russel, George   R130
Russel, Leven   2309
Russel, Robert jr   2447
Russel, William   2654, R152,
  R255
Russell, Andrew   2577
Russell (Russel), Matthew
  1874, 2048
Russell (Russel), Robert   2183,
  2692
Russell (Russel), Timothy
  2296, 2440
Ryan, James   2569
Sanders, Hezekiah   2127,
  2344, 2497
Sanders, James   2036, 2153,
  2233, 2335
Sanders, James sr   R232, R233
Sanders, Joel   1937, 2304,
  2591, 2647, 2688, 2762
Sanders, John   2101, 2402,
  2640, R233
Sanders, John sr   2304
Sanders, Stephen   1976
Saners, John jr   2127
Sarratt, James   1955, 1956,
  2756

Sarratt (Sarrat), John   1910,
  1956, 2790, 2969
Saunders, James   2011, 2012,
  2014
Saundors, Francis   2003
Savage, Zachariah   2001
Savage, widow   1946
Scales, Henry   2244, R100
Scales, James   2215
Scales, John   2222
Scissna, Stephen   2559
Scorden, John   R122
Scot, Jacob   1868
Scott, Andrew   1979
Scott, Elisabeth   2609
Scott, Matthew   2144
Scott, William   1978, 2203
Scott, Elizabeth   2807
Scurry, Ely   2237, R247
Scurry, Susannah   R171
Scury, Martin   R150
Scury, widow   R112
Seales, Henry (Henery)   2094,
  R123, R147, R228
Seales, John   2222, R170
Self,   2139
Self, William   R97
Sellers, Philip   2081
Selman (Selmun), Benjamin
  2241, 2294
Semon, John   2490
Sermon, Benjamin   2668
Settle, William   2043
Setts, James   2080
Sevings, Matthias   2586
Sexton, Thomas   2664
Shaimuher,   2448
Shannon, Hugh   2321
Shannon, William   2380, 2382
Sharp, Samuel   R239
Sharpe, Anthony   2582, 2583,
  2584, 2585, 2586, 2587
Shatterlin, Andrew   2353
Shatterlings, Michael   1859

Shaver, William   2532, 2656
Shaw,   2756
Shaw, Benjamin   2370
Shaw, Findley   1905, 1938
Shaw, Finley   2332
Shaw, Hugh   1879, 2080
Shaw, John   2650
Shaw, Philip   2735
Shaw, Robert   1906, 1907,
   2236, 2316, 2455
Shaw, Saml   2080
Shaw, William   1879, 1906,
   2117, 2316, 2575, 2616
Shearer,   1857
Shearer, David   2751, 2752
Shearer, Jacob   2204, 2909
Shearer, Jacob D   2531
Shearer, William jr   2748
Shearwood, Daniel   2576, 2607
Sheaver, David   2872
Sheaver, William   2869
Sheaver, William jr   2748
Shefferd, Willm   2370
Shelley, James   2763
Shelley, Jeremiah   2339, 2340,
   2585, 2587
Shelley, John   2622
Shelley, Nathan   1917
Shepherd, John   R182, R164
Sherk (Shrk), Andrew   2205
Sherwood, Hugh   2755
Shew (Shew, Show), Philip
   2027, 2734, 2735, 2856
Shirk, Andrew   2561
Shitterling, Michael   2565
Shoemake, Joshua   R264
Shoemaker, Susannah   2463
Shoemaker, widow   2672
Shoffner, George   2735
Shopshear, Winkfield   2177,
   2178
Short, Moses   2491
Short, Moses sr   R210
Short, Oldham   R103

Short, Samuel   2083, 2348,
   R200
Short, William A   2354
Short, widow   1916, 2354
Shropshere, Wirkfield   2111
Shropshiar, St. John   R147
Shurwood, Daniel   2598, 2796
Silfon, Wm   2154
Simmerman,   2463
Simmons (Simmings,
   Smnnons), John   2067, 2148,
   2217, R145
Simpson, Nathan   2863
Simpson, Nathaniel   2337,
   2519, 2692, 2742
Simpson, Peter R   2633, 2830
Simpson, Richard   1900
Simpson, Thomas   R209
Simson, Peter B   2694
Singleton,   2157
Sinnen, Stephen   2846
Sisney, Stephen   2652
Slatkas, George   1975
Small, Robert   1962, 1963,
   1964, 2089, 2158, 2193,
   R98, R145, R146, R161,
   R162, R169, R186
Smith,   2096
Smith, Andr   2617
Smith, Benjamin   2711, R181
Smith, Drury   2058, 2174
Smith, Frederick   2732
Smith, James   2969
Smith, John   1924, 1931,
   1948, 2115, 2321, 2332,
   2746, R152
Smith, John P   2568
Smith, Joshua   2174, 2175,
   2176, 2215
Smith, Peter   2479, 2533, 2695
Smith, Richard   R240
Smith, Robert   1927
Smith, Samuel   2126
Smith, William   1936, 2195

Sneed, Alexander   R163, R228
Sools, Jacob   2586
Soots, Adam   2749
Sotethrland,   2013
Southerland, William   R226
Spear, Theophilous   2152
Spencer, Abraham   1911, R196
Spere,   2042
Speres, William   2001
Springer, Uriah   2696
Sprout,   R208
Spruce, John   2709
Spruce, John H   2634, 2702, 2831
Spruce (Sprus), William   1948, 2709
Spurrier, Theophelous   R111
Stack,   2743
Stack, Elijah   2509
Stafford, John   2675
Stafford, William   2248, 2251, 2368, 2432
Standfield, John   2763
Stanley, Elijah   1976
Stanley (Standley), John   2469, 2470, 2556, 2964
Stanley (Standley), Joseph   1998, 2647, 2688, 2842
Stanley, Stangeman   2370
Star, Jacob   2265
Starbuck, Gager   2398, 2399
Starbuck, William   1950, 1981
Starr, Adam   1864, 1865, 2016, 2748, 2899, 2901
Starrat, John   2707, 2875, 2891, 2911, 2936
Starratt, John   2392
Stawhon, Moses   1999
Stephens, Evan   2754
Stephens, Peter   2262
Stephens, widow   R265
Stephenson, John   2613, 2811
Steplow, William   2024
Steven,   1901

Stevenson, John   2493
Stevenson, Mathew   2613
Steward, John   2428
Stewart (Stuart), Findley   2010, 2080, 2660
Stewart, George   2116, 2263, 2359
Stewart, John   2255, 2256, 2312, 2355, 2382, 2598, 2637, 2680
Stewart, Thomas   2407, 2409
Stockard, John   R249
Stokes, Thomas   2715
Stone, Benjamin   2279
Stone, Burges (Burgis)   R248, R262
Stone, John   1941, 2379, 2774
Story, Caleb   2543
Strahan, Moses   2317
Strahorn,   2213
Strain, John   1863
Stratton, William   R153
Strawhon,   2187
Stricker, Garrard   2528
Stricklin (Stricklain, Strickland), Jacob   1873, 2171, 2414
Stricklin, Jacob   2542, 2557
Stricklin, Jacob sr   1922
Stricklin, John   2170
Strong, James   2094, 2244
Strong, John   R135
Struker, Garnet   2091
Stublefield (Stubblefield), Edward   2057, R237
Stublefield, Wyatt   R203
Suit, Jacob   2684
Sulivan (Sullivand),   2717, 2750
Sulivan (Sulivant), Fletcher   2736, 2770, 2785, 2857, 2877
Sulivant, Samuel   1951
Sullivan (Sillivan), Charles

2967

Sullivan (Salivan, Sulivan),
Daniel   2629, 2637

Sullivan (Silivan), Florence
2594, 2736

Sullivan (Sulivant), Jenkin
(Ginkin)   2717, 2718, 2781,
2782

Summer, Peter   2611

Summerman, George   2072,
2455, 2456

Summers,   2448, 2644

Summers (Sumers), Jacob
2080, 2448, 2463

Summers, Wm   2617

Suth, John   2321

Sutherland,   2107

Sutherlin, John   1892

Suton,   2768

Suttle, David   2254

Sutz, Adam   2968

Swaim (Sweim), William
2109, 2866

Swain,   2743

Swam, widow   2576

Swean, Joseph   2552

Sweet, John   2224, 2457

Sweper, Jacob   2143

Swesser, Jacob   2143

Swim,   2775

Swim, Michael   1909

Swim, Salley   2740

Swim, William   1909, 2744,
2745

Swing, John   2684, 2889

Swing, Matthew   1868

Swing, Matthias   2643, 2684,
2691

Swinnon, John   2148

Swisher, Francis   2733, 2757

Swisher, Jacob jr   2757

Swisher, John   2757

Taggals,   2129

Talbot, John   2381, 2545

Tall, Christian   2810

Tasey, Alexander   2464

Tasey, Martha   2464, 2623,
2820

Tate,   1875

Tate, Adam   R125

Tate, John   1882

Tate, Zepheniah   2520

Tatom,   R134

Tatom (Tatum), Edward   2361

Tatum, John   2361

Tayler, Richard   2002

Taylor,   2563

Taylor (Tailor), John   2298,
2460

Taylor, John H   2042

Taylor, Joseph   2030, 2164

Taylor, Reuben   R199

Taylor, Thomas   2167, 2589

Tedford, Robert   2603

Terrell, Micaijah   2556

Thacker (Thacher), Nathan
1995, 2266

Thacker, Zachariah   1995

Tharpar, John   2186

Thomas, James   R263

Thomas, John   2063, 2176,
2188

Thomas, Michael   2065, 2168

Thomas, William   2375

Thombury, Thos   2574

Thompson,   2299

Thompson (Thomson),
Ephraim   2385, R193, R106,
R213, R259

Thompson, James   2397, 2610,
2808

Thompson, Robert   2346,
2595, 2632, 2685, 2766,
2829

Thompson, Samuel   2346

Thoras, James   2700

Thornburg, David   2695

Thornburg (Thornberry,

Wilson (Willson), Andrew
2032, 2141, 2894, 2961
Wilson, Daniel   2244
Wilson, George   2651, 2891
Wilson, James   1970, 2160,
2275
Wilson, John   2206
Wilson, Jonathan   2675
Wilson (Willson), Joseph   2487
Wilson, Michael   2486, 2649
Wilson, Rachel   2392
Wilson, Richard   2257, 2438
Wilson, William   2031
Winigh, Daniel   2612
Witt, Michael (Micael)   2142,
2143, 2732, 2733, 2757,
2759, 2853, 2854
Wolfington, James   2653
Wolfington, John   2122, 2640,
2653, 2836
Woodburn, Thomas   2767
Woods,   1863
Woods, William   1855
Woodside, John   1862
Worick, Jacob   2459
Work (Works), Henry   2004,
2728
Work, James   2621, 2728
Worth, David   2483
Worth, Francis   2134, 2251
Worth, Joseph   2774
Wrecker, John   2402
Wright, Adam   2696
Wright, Edward   2492, 2522
Wright, Ezekiel   R109
Wright, Francis   2124, R237
Wright, Isaac   2132, 2133,
2292
Wright, James   2013, 2015,
2015, 2023, 2392, 2500,
R204, R249
Wright, James jr   1904
Wright, James sr   1904
Wright, Joshua   2387, 2410,

R90
Wright, Leven   1894
Wright, Prudence   R217, R218
Wright, Thos   2559
Wyatt, George   2850
Wyrick (Wyruk), Martin
2726, 2732
Yoeman, Drury   R99
Yoeman, Stokes   R99
Young, Francis   2049, 2118
Young, Jesse   R216
Young, John   2082, R198
Young, William   1971, 1972,
2288, R244
Yours, William   R249

Geographical locations:
Assembly, General   R265
Bent, Niles   2415
Branch, Bare   2108
Branch, Blackwood   2196
Branch, Bobbs   2312
Branch, Brushy   2089
Branch, Cabbin   1999, 2317
Branch, Camp   2158, 2223
Branch, Ceader   2201
Branch, Crooked   2664
Branch, Fuggals   2129
Branch, Glady   2158, R98
Branch, Gleady   1964
Branch, Gumping   2466
Branch, Hay   2367
Branch, Hays   1932
Branch, Hazel   2086
Branch, Hockey   1958
Branch, Horsepin   1983
Branch, J. Walker's   2327
Branch, Jumping   R94
Branch, Kings   R106, R107,
R259
Branch, Lick   1918, 1921,
2138
Branch, Little Buffalo   2159,
2162

2542, 2566, 2590, 2651,
2713
Creek, Buffalo Island   2052,
2175, 2176, 2177, 2178,
2375, R135, R147, R163,
R180, R191, R219, R225,
R228, R253, R254
Creek, Burch   2638
Creek, Cedar (Ceder)   1942,
1969, 2242
Creek, Chesnut   1956
Creek, Clarks   1961
Creek, Clouds   R122
Creek, Corbeys   2262
Creek, County line   2298
Creek, Curbys   R124, R229
Creek, D. Ozburn's   2678
Creek, Danels   2662
Creek, Double   1997, 2059
Creek, Falls   2051, 2274
Creek, Fishers   R110, R138
Creek, Fishing   2219, R192,
R197
Creek, Giles   1956
Creek, Gileses   2163
Creek, Glady   R161
Creek, Great Alamance   1864,
1865, 1879, 1905, 1906,
1907, 1938, 1952, 1969,
1974, 1985, 2010, 2041,
2048, 2115, 2242, 2261,
2323, 2562, 2565, 2584,
2618, 2660, 2708, 2748,
2749
Creek, Harris   2644
Creek, Hickory   1928, 1933,
1967, 2070, 2228, 2249,
2252, 2287, 2297, 2313,
2314, 2315, 2343, 2408,
2458, 2505, 2515, 2552,
2572, 2582, 2583, 2601,
2610, 2674
Creek, Hogans (Hogens)
1858, 1903, 1946, 1980,

1988, 1995, 2001, 2020,
2022, 2043, 2054, 2061,
2065, 2071, 2075, 2088,
2103, 2105, 2107, 2120,
2121, 2155, 2156, 2168,
2191, 2216, 2230, 2239,
2266, 2321, 2326, 2410,
2411, 2418, 2518, R90, R91,
R101, R115, R134, R144,
R244
Creek, Horsepen   1899, 2117,
2136, 2247, 2267, 2289,
2296, 2363, 2365, 2427,
2440, 2540, 2574, 2652
Creek, Izeal   2677
Creek, Jacobs   1867, 1890,
1902, 1920, 2000, 2049,
2060, 2063, 2076, 2077,
2123, 2189, 2192, 2253,
2347, 2348, 2349, 2383,
2385, 2424, 2485, 2491,
R93, R96, R103, R114,
R133, R141, R142, R145,
R149, R149, R150, R156,
R158, R159, R164, R176,
R182, R184, R186, R200,
R216, R243, R249, R257,
R262
Creek, Kerbeys (Kerbies)
2401, 2050
Creek, Land   2359
Creek, Lawrences   2019
Creek, Little Alamance   1945,
2226, 2256, 2780
Creek, Little Buffalo   2025
Creek, Little Hickory   2377,
2378, 2443
Creek, Little Rockhouse   2225,
2240, 2309, 2310, R140,
R250
Creek, Little Stinking Quarter
2525, 2696
Creek, Little Town   2148,
2217, 2218

Creek, Little Troublesome
1858, 1979, 2411, R153
Creek, Londons   R240
Creek, Matrimony   2040,
2090, 2159, 2162, 2198,
2371, R179
Creek, Mill   R207
Creek, Moons   1984, 2300,
2510, 2793
Creek, Moores   1860, 2389
Creek, Mordicais   2272, 2444,
2445, 2473, 2476, 2526,
2653
Creek, Moses   2237, R166,
R171, R247
Creek, Mosses   R112, R113
Creek, Muddy   2523
Creek, N Buffalo   1908, 1944,
2221, 2264, 2406, 2472,
2492, 2522, 2538, 2540,
2554, 2563, 2602, 2706,
2707, 2709, 2710, 2758,
2761, 2776
Creek, N. Larimer's   2498
Creek, Pawpaw (Paupau,
Poppow)   2051, 2058, 2174,
2416
Creek, Peony   2165
Creek, Piney   1992, 1993,
2032, 2039, 2067, 2104
Creek, Piney   2292, R161,
R162, R227
Creek, Pole Cat   1871, 1941,
1986, 2109, 2255, 2287,
2305, 2355, 2379, 2382,
2384, 2405, 2412, 2436,
2486, 2505, 2515, 2576,
2604, 2607, 2629, 2630,
2637, 2649, 2665, 2680,
2712, 2723,   2724, 2740,
2744, 2745, 2755, 2774,
2775, 2779
Creek, Porters   2756
Creek, Quarquaw (Quacquaw,

Quagua)   2238, R143, R178
Creek, Reeds   2026, 2222,
2516, R170, R172
Creek, Richland   1982, 2122,
2257, 2303, 2311, 2329,
2407, 2409, 2444, 2450,
2705
Creek, Rock   1857, 1924,
2091, 2116, 2204, 2342,
2403, 2528, 2531, 2532,
2768
Creek, Rockey   1930, 2200
Creek, Rockhouse   1866,
1962, 1990, 1991, 2003,
2014, 2038, 2082, 2086,
2087, 2108, 2131, 2135,
2152, 2153, 2185, 2220,
2225, 2294, 2318, 2335,
2351, 2374, 2391, R111,
R116, R117, R149, R232
Creek, Rose (Roses)   1910,
1955
Creek, Rosses   2392
Creek, Ruddocks (Reddocks,
Rudduckses)   1887, 2271,
2433, 2468, 2503, 2537,
2581
Creek, Ryans   2248
Creek, S Buffalo   1870, 1872,
1873, 1883, 1884, 1916,
1922, 1951, 2073, 2160,
2161, 2170, 2171, 2271,
2293, 2296, 2405, 2467,
2469, 2492, 2509, 2514,
2522, 2540, 2550, 2577,
2596, 2599, 2600, 2628,
2634, 2648, 2687, 2702,
2710, 2730, 2743, 2778,
2783
Creek, Sandy (Sandey)   2436,
2686
Creek, Shepherds   2181
Creek, Shockleys   1859
Creek, Still house   2135

1886, 1891, 1897, 1901,
1915, 1925, 1926, 1932,
1936, 1953, 1958, 1978,
1981, 1983, 1998, 1999,
2002, 2009, 2021, 2035,
2053, 2125, 2126, 2142,
2143, 2182, 2187, 2195,
2213, 2232, 2299, 2317,
2331, 2337, 2346, 2359,
2364, 2369, 2370, 2376,
2386, 2398, 2399, 2402,
2419, 2421, 2425, 2426,
2459, 2472, 2475, 2480,
2499, 2500, 2519, 2534,
2535, 2536, 2554, 2567,
2592, 2593, 2595, 2597,
2621, 2623, 2626, 2632,
2633, 2636, 2642, 2647,
2654, 2670, 2671, 2685,
2688, 2692, 2715, 2726,
2732, 2733, 2738, 2742,
2756, 2757, 2759, 2760,
2766
Fork, Rich   2295, 2449, 2453,
2544, 2606, 2646, 2727,
2747
Fork, Ridge (Ridge)   2447,
2617
Fork, Rocky   R95
Fork, second Rich   2471, 2474
Fork, Silver   2280, 2281
Fork, Stones   1888, 2129
Fork, Tomlins   2176
Fork, Town   2220
Fork, White oak   2111, 2177,
2178, R147
Governors,   R114
Hill, Piney   R168
Hill, Whetston   R158
Ironworks,   2032, 2193,
2223, 2308
Level, Chork   R178
Mill, Dillion's   1966
Moravian,   2254

NC, Guilford Co   R172
NC, New Garden   2381
NC, Orange Co   2580, 2735,
2760
NC, Randolph Co   2430, 2719,
2725, 2739, 2788, 2790
NC, Rowan Co   2306, 2341
NC, Salisbury   1877
NC, Springfield   2523, 2569
NC, Surry Co   2015, 2028,
2053,   2190, 2274
River, Dan   1877, 1960, 2052,
2055, 2056, 2083, 2090,
2098, 2132, 2133, 2147,
2179, 2262, 2330, 2356,
2371, 2415, 2489, 2490,
R99, R102, R155, R165,
R220, R229, R230, R245,
R261, R264, R265
River, Deep   1894, 1937,
1940, 1947, 1957, 1975,
1976, 1977, 2005, 2035,
2068, 2101, 2110, 2127,
2166, 2186, 2188, 2202,
2207, 2208, 2209, 2214,
2224, 2204, 2307, 2312,
2338, 2344, 2350, 2358,
2360, 2366, 2372, 2378,
2381, 2397, 2404, 2420,
2425, 2429, 2431, 2432,
2433, 2439, 2441, 2442,
2450, 2452, 2482, 2483,
2486, 2495, 2506, 2507,
2508, 2511, 2512, 2513,
2520, 2527, 2529, 2530,
2545, 2570, 2591, 2619,
2620, 2622, 2624, 2625,
2641, 2645, 2667, 2675,
2679, 2725, 2729, 2737,
2739, 2741, 2762, 2763,
2764, 2773, 2784
River, Haw   1863, 1891, 1896,
1897, 1900, 1910, 1918,
1932, 1954, 1956, 1981,

www.ingramcontent.com/pod-product-compliance
Lightning Source LLC
Chambersburg PA
CBHW021832020426
42334CB00014B/591